Praise for *The One Peaceful World Cookbook*

"Imagine eating the most delicious food and, as a consequence, finding yourself restored to good health and optimal weight, galvanized with more energy, blessed with more beauty, and elevated to a joyful and better you. That's what *The One Peaceful World Cookbook* can give you. Learn from the wisdom in its pages, apply its easy-to-follow recipes, eat the delicious food, and enjoy your beautiful life."

—**TOM MONTE**, bestselling author or coauthor of more than 35 books, including *Unexpected Recoveries* and *Recalled by Life*

"I can't count the number of times people ask me what 'macrobiotics' is. These pages bring to life just how friendly, easy, delicious, and nutritionally sound the macrobiotic lifestyle is. This is a masterpiece and a must-have for anyone interested in luscious, healthy cooking . . . in other words, everybody!"

—**CHRISTINA PIRELLO**, bestselling author and Emmy-award-winning host of *Christina Cooks*

"Sachi's passion for art, beauty, and cooking shines through in her exciting new cookbook. Her photography is simply stunning, bringing the dishes to life, inspiring the reader to get in the kitchen and try the recipes. Sachi's attention to detail is what makes her cooking so outstanding!"

—**WARREN KRAMER**, macrobiotic counselor, lecturer, and cooking teacher

"Beautiful, tasty, and healthy—the credo for macrobiotic food—convincingly presented by Sachi Kato and Alex Jack in *The One Peaceful World Cookbook*. The joy of cooking acquires a deeper meaning with this attractive manual. The superbly illustrated recipes and use of the different foods will help many people on their path to a better quality of life."

—**WIEKE NELISSEN**, codirector of the Kushi Institute of Europe

"Alex Jack and Sachi Kato have produced a wonderful book that is a pleasure for both the mind and the eye. Building on the foundation of macrobiotic nutrition and cooking, they offer a completely modern update with presentation of useful and practical information for creating a healthy diet and way of life. I highly recommend this book for any kitchen or library."

—**BILL TARA**, MACROVegan Center in Ireland

"*The One Peaceful World Cookbook* is a beautiful stroll through the healing of modern diseases with healthy food. There are ample recipes for whole meals, snacks, and condiments to make eating delicious food new and exciting. The pictures are inspiring and recipes easy to follow. Get ready to reclaim and maintain your health!"

—**JANE TEAS**, scientific and medical researcher at the South Carolina Cancer Center

"Alex Jack and Sachi Kato have created more than an attractive cookbook. Their new book demonstrates the beauty and diversity of delicious and healthy vegan, macrobiotic cuisine. It also offers valuable insight into the principles and philosophy underlying this way of eating, cooking, and living."

—**DENNY WAXMAN**, founder of the Strengthening Health Institute
and author of *The Complete Macrobiotic Diet*

"*The One Peaceful World Cookbook* is a perfect vegan, macrobiotic guide and resource filled with extraordinary research and nutritious, delicious recipes created by two gifted authors, Alex Jack and Sachi Kato. This book can significantly improve your health and well-being!"

—**JUDY MACKENNEY**, macrobiotic counselor, teacher, and cancer survivor

"*The One Peaceful World Cookbook* is a must-read because of its clarity, comprehensive approach, great recipes, and beautiful design. Its combination of theory and practice make it invaluable."

—**FRANCISCO VARATOJO**, macrobiotic teacher and
director of the Macrobiotic Institute of Portugal

"Developing an intuitive eye for cooking using foods from the earth is one of the highest art forms. I think *The One Peaceful World Cookbook* covers the breadth and scope of macrobiotic cooking in such a way as to accomplish this goal. The synergistic literary works of Alex Jack and the uniquely talented photos and creative recipes of Sachi Kato bring a treasure that is sure to inspire and reawaken our memory that we are what we eat. The pages sizzle with creative energy. Anyone interested in their health and the health of this planet will find this masterpiece a keeper."

—**SHERI-LYNN DEMARIS M.ED.**, macrobiotic cooking teacher
and author of *Macro Magic for Kids and Parents*

"In their original form, all cereal grains project delicate awns from their heads. Like antennae, the awns reach toward the Milky Way and beyond toward the infinite universe, channeling the light and energy of health, peace, and unlimited freedom. *The One Peaceful World Cookbook* is a guide-book to bringing that energy to your daily table. Use it with care and wisdom."

—**EDWARD ESKO**, author of *One Peaceful Universe*

"Inspired by Michio Kushi's vision of a world at peace, Alex Jack and Sachi Kato offer old macro-biotic favorites with intriguing twists alongside sparkling new creations—all with a keen atten-tion to twenty-first-century issues and a comprehensive vision to guide both beginning journeyer and well-versed traveler on their culinary journey."

—**CATHERINE L. ALBANESE**, J.F. Rowny Professor Emerita in Comparative Religions
and Research Professor, University of California, Santa Barbara,
and Level IV Graduate, Kushi Institute

"Alex Jack and Sachi Kato will inspire you with their immense knowledge on how to live life to the full. Through their knowledge and passion for health, nutrition, and life philosophy, you will be able to gather the tools to allow you to steer in a new and positive direction. A beautiful book that's a must for every household."

—**MARLENE WATSON-TARA**, cooking teacher and
author of *Macrobiotics for All Seasons*

"We both felt such excitement when we opened *The One Peaceful World Cookbook*! The delicious recipes, so beautifully photographed by author, Sachi Kato, reignited our great and enduring enthusiasm for these healing, delicious, and ecological macrobiotic dishes that she so expertly prepares and teaches. Alex Jack, famed author and devoted macrobiotic educator, joins powerfully with chef, Sachi Kato, in creating this breathtaking guide to a more healthy, balanced, and happy life through a conscious and joyous vegan macrobiotic regime."

—**LINO AND JANE Q. STANCHICH**, macrobiotic authors
and educators, GreatLifeGlobal.com

"Kind of in awe of this book. The ultimate vegan/macrobiotic cookbook for everyone interested in not only delicious and doable recipes but those seeking healthy and even healing cuisines. Beautiful pictures and a great layout from long-time educator Alex Jack and macrobiotic cook Sachi Kato . . . Would highly recommend it to everyone, from those looking to just add more grains and vegetables to their diets to casual vegetarians looking to expand their veggie horizons."

—**NADINE BARNER**, macrobiotic counselor,
educator and private chef based in Los Angeles

"A feast for your eyes and senses, this amazing cookbook, with modern day macrobiotic dishes, dispels the brown rice macrobiotic myth! Healthy food doesn't come any tastier than this! With Alex's wealth of knowledge and Sachi's passion for cooking, this is a must for anyone interested in eating in a healthy way."

—**DAVID AND NICOLA MCCARTHY**, Kushi Macrobiotic School, UK

"*Exciting* is the word that comes to mind upon reading *The One Peaceful World Cookbook*. The contemporary art of vegan, macrobiotic cooking is celebrated in the 150+ creative international recipes that are clearly expressed, making them accessible to all. Vibrant close-up color photos, taken by global chef Sachi Kato, accompany the recipes. They inspire the reader to easily envision making the dishes. Recipes span the plant-based menu from soups to whole grains (from Spanish paella to Italian risotto to Asian dumplings), and vegetables, including sea veggies and salads, to beans and other 'green proteins,' to fermented foods, desserts, and natural remedies. Foodies, as well as people seeking support in their plant-based lifestyle, will benefit greatly as they integrate this cutting-edge cookbook's treasures into their daily lives."

—**MEREDITH MCCARTY**, award-winning cookbook author
and nutrition educator, healingcuisine.com

"*The One Peaceful World Cookbook* is a delightful guide full of important information for people who are new to macrobiotics. It also contains splendid recipes with beautiful photos for everyone who seeks variety in their meals. I truly enjoyed this book. Bravo to Alex and Sachi."

—**SANAE SUZUKI, BFRP**, whole health macrobiotic counselor and
author of *Love, Sanae* and *Healthy Happy Pooch*

Fried Rice-Vermicelli
(see recipe on page 76)

THE ONE PEACEFUL WORLD COOKBOOK

OVER 150 VEGAN, MACROBIOTIC RECIPES FOR VIBRANT HEALTH AND HAPPINESS

Contemporary Whole-Food Cooking and Natural Remedies

ALEX JACK AND SACHI KATO

BenBella Books, Inc.
Dallas, TX

BenBella

BenBella Books, Inc.
10440 N. Central Expressway, Suite 800 | Dallas, TX 75231
www.benbellabooks.com | Send feedback to feedback@benbellabooks.com

Printed in the United States of America
10 9 8 7 6 5 4 3 2 1

Library of Congress Cataloging-in-Publication Data:
Names: Jack, Alex, 1945- author. | Kato, Sachi, author.
Title: The one peaceful world cookbook : over 150 vegan macrobiotic recipes
   for vibrant health and happiness : contemporary whole-food cooking and
   natural remedies / by Alex Jack and Sachi Kato.
Description: Dallas, TX : BenBella Books, Inc., [2017]
Identifiers: LCCN 2016056091 (print) | LCCN 2016058143 (ebook) | ISBN
   9781944648244 (trade paper) | ISBN 9781944648251 (electronic)
Subjects: LCSH: Macrobiotic diet—Recipes. | Cooking, Japanese. | Natural
   foods. | Functional foods. | Holistic medicine. | LCGFT: Cookbooks.
Classification: LCC RM235 .J335 2017 (print) | LCC RM235 (ebook) | DDC
   641.5/636—dc23
LC record available at https://lccn.loc.gov/2016056091

Editing by Laurel Leigh Erdoiza
Copyediting by Nicole Brugger-Dethmers
Proofreading by Sarah Vostok and
   Cape Cod Compositors, Inc.
Indexing by WordCo Indexing Services, Inc.
Text design and composition by
   Silver Feather Design

Cover design by Sarah Avinger
Cover photography by Sachi Kato
Interior photography by Sachi Kato
Printed by Versa Press

Distributed by Perseus Distribution
www.perseusdistribution.com

To place orders through Perseus Distribution:
Tel: (800) 343-4499 | Fax: (800) 351-5073
E-mail: orderentry@perseusbooks.com

Special discounts for bulk sales (minimum of 25 copies) are available.
Please contact Aida Herrera at aida@benbellabooks.com.

In memory of Michio and Aveline Kushi, and dedicated to humanity's endless dream of one healthy, peaceful world.

"The simplest dishes are the hardest to make. The highest art in cooking is the preparation of a bowl of rice."

—MICHIO KUSHI

Miso Soup
(see recipe on page 99)

CONTENTS

We all have come from infinity,
We all live within infinity,
We all shall return to infinity,
We are all manifestation of
            one infinity,
We are all brothers and sisters of
                one infinite universe,
Let us love each other,
Let us help each other,
Let us encourage each other,
Let us all together continue to realize
The endless dream of
            one peaceful world,
We are always one forever.

                    Michio Kushi
                    久司道夫

First Light

THE FLAME OF LIFE

"The secret for health and wisdom, freedom and happiness—all physical, mental, and spiritual as well as social well-being—is in front of us, day to day, lying in every dish we consume. Learning how to choose foods, how to cook balanced meals, and how to eat wisely provides the most central answers to the question of our destiny as human beings."

—MICHIO KUSHI

For thousands of generations, the hearth served as the focal point, as well as the sacred altar, for the family, clan, or tribe. In ancient Rome, a flame from the hearth of Vesta, the goddess of the kitchen, home, and family, was taken to establish new colonies and outposts. The I Ching, or Book of Change, compared itself to a *ding*, a bronze cauldron in which millet, rice, and other foods were cooked over an open flame and offered to heaven. As the ancient Chinese classic instructs: "The wood serves as nourishment for the flame, the spirit. All that is visible must grow beyond itself, extend into the realm of the invisible. Thereby it receives its true consecration and clarity and takes firm root in the cosmic order."[1]

Today, continuity with the flame that kindled, nourished, and sustained the human family has been lost. For thousands of years, wood served as the principal fuel. Only during the last millennium has it been replaced by coal, gas, oil, or other more concentrated natural sources of energy. Today, electric, microwave, induction, and other artificial sources of heat—often powered by nuclear energy—prevail. Along with chemically treated, highly processed "junk food," these new synthetic or "junk flames" produce an abnormally high or low energy and chaotic vibrations that separate us from the natural fire that has sustained all past eras.

As the highest art, macrobiotic or whole-foods cooking over a calm, peaceful, sustainable fire enables us to rediscover and reconnect with the flame of life. It gives us the physical strength and vitality, emotional balance, and mental and spiritual clarity to meet the challenges of the age and pass on our life and spirit to future generations.

---

[1] Richard Wilhelm and Cary F. Baynes, trans., *The I Ching, or, Book of Changes* (Princeton, NJ: Princeton University Press, 1967.)

FOREWORD

I still remember the first cooking class I had with Sachi Kato. We all sat behind a table in her kitchen in Los Angeles while she showed us how to make beautiful, creamy squash soup with shiitake broth, millet mash, and blanched vegetables with tahini dill dressing. And, of course, amazing melon kanten! I was captivated by the sweet, complex flavors and smells and by the way Sachi so elegantly prepared the food. I never knew that plant-based cooking could be this diverse, delicious, and unique. The food, just like Sachi herself, felt larger than life. From that day on, Sachi became one of my favorite macrobiotic chefs and someone I turn to when I'm looking for a new recipe.

Since that time I have learned much more about the macrobiotic way of life and its unique take on cooking, lifestyle, and healing philosophies. My journeys have brought me to the Kushi Institute on more than one occasion, giving me an opportunity to meet and study with Alex Jack, and learn from him ancient concepts of healing that have changed the way I look at the human body and have shaped my medical practice.

Now as an integrative and functional medicine physician specializing in culinary medicine, I have witnessed firsthand the power food can have on illness and the general quality of life. By re-entering the kitchen and preparing whole foods, primarily plant-based, we begin to nourish ourselves and our families on a level that promotes cellular regeneration, appreciation for life and others, and a general sense of well-being. As an initial "prescription" for my patients I provide dietary recommendations with specific vegetables, teas, soups, and whole grains to support their healing journey. Some of those recipes can be found in this book.

But there are challenges. In my practice I have witnessed all too often how people don't know how to cook or simply don't make the time to prepare meals for themselves or their families. Many factors contribute to this, including a lack of confidence and a lack of knowledge. A common challenge is how to cook without the use of saturated and trans fats, dairy, and sugar. Or even knowing the proper tools needed for setting up your kitchen. Recipes handed down by generations are getting lost, and albeit not always healthy; the skills required to cook in general are dulled.

It's a dangerous social trend. According to a recent survey of 3,000 adults by Morgan Stanley, about 53 percent of millennials say they eat at restaurants at least once a week, compared with 43 percent of Generation X or baby boomers.[1] For the first time ever, in 2014 Americans spent more money on food away from home than food prepared and consumed at home,

---

[1] "AlphaWise Survey: What Millennials Want . . ." Morgan Stanley Research, March 24, 2015. http://static.ow.ly/docs/Millennials%20Morgan%20Stanley_3r3Z.pdf.

according to the US Department of Agriculture's Economic Research Service (ERS).[2] In 1960, when JFK was elected president, Americans spent just 26 percent of their incomes on food away from home. The gap has almost doubled over time.

The reality is that not only does eating away from home detract from family and self-empowerment; it's not a substitute for healthy cooking in your own home. Even in the "healthiest" restaurants, we have no control over the amount of salt, sugars, and other ingredients added to our meal, which are often used in the extreme.

Macrobiotics takes these often-ignored specifics into account. Since I began exploring its concepts, such as yin and yang, in the context of these extreme foods, like salt, sugar, animal foods, and alcohol, it has changed the way I look at illness and the macrobiotic approach to healing. Macrobiotics is the most balanced, satisfying, and holistic method of enjoying meals. And learning methods such as planning balanced meals and proper food preparation can change health and allow us to heal from within.

This book is an amazing guide to taking that first step. *The One Peaceful World Cookbook* not only provides us with high-end, innovative plant-based recipes, but also with a full philosophical and educational guide for bringing us back to the kitchen, a focal point for family and community and a way to take charge of your health. It is also a wonderful homage to Michio and Aveline Kushi and their dream of one healthy, peaceful world.

I am honored to be a part of this work, and I am excited to be able to share this comprehensive guide with my patients and my family.

—SOMMER WHITE, MD
Nashville, Tennessee

---

[2] "U.S. Food-Away-from-Home_Sales_Topped-Food-at-Home Sales in 2014," United States Department of Agriculture, Economic Research Services. Last modified April 12, 2016. https://www.ers.usda.gov/data-products/chart-gallery/gallery/chart-detail/?chartId=58364.

INTRODUCTION

"We all share and are nourished by one common planet, the earth. For thousands of generations, most of the human family has lived together in relative harmony on this small sphere as it spirals through space. Before the spreading rays of the dawn and under the revolving canopy of the Northern Sky, millennia of parents, children, and other family members have shared the harvest and saved seeds to plant the following spring."

—*One Peaceful World* by Michio Kushi with Alex Jack

In *One Peaceful World: Creating a Healthy and Harmonious Mind, Home, and World Community*, Michio Kushi describes how as a young man he visited Hiroshima shortly after the atomic bombing. He lived in the city as a child, and the utter devastation he witnessed moved him to devote his life to creating a world of enduring peace. In macrobiotics, the young political science graduate of Tokyo University found a practical method to realize this dream.

The roots of macrobiotics go back to Hippocrates, who coined the term from Greek roots that mean "long life" or "great life." The father of medicine's approach to health and healing can be summarized in his own famous proverb, "Let food be thy medicine and thy medicine be food." At the end of World War II, Michio came to the United States to pursue his studies in world peace and international order. Over the next half century, he unified the traditional wisdom of the East with the practical technology of the West. In an era poised on the brink of nuclear war and the spread of heart disease, cancer, and other chronic disorders, Michio taught modern society that organic farming and a balanced natural foods diet were the keys to recovering and managing our daily health and well-being and living together in peace and harmony. In thousands of speeches, seminars and classes, and personal consultations, his underlying message reflected the common dream of all humanity—the realization of "One Peaceful World"—through peaceful biological and spiritual change.

As the pioneers of the modern natural foods movement, Michio and his wife Aveline and their associates introduced and popularized organically grown whole foods meals featuring flavorful miso soups; whole grains; tasty noodles and pasta; energizing tofu, tempeh, seitan, and other green-protein dishes; a cornucopia of fresh vegetables; delectable sea vegetables; and other nourishing, predominantly plant-based foods. Today these foods are going mainstream and changing the way the people of America—and the world—eat, heal, and relate to one another.

A balanced plant-based way of eating has enhanced the lives of millions of people on the planet. It has enabled them to maintain their basic health and vitality. It has helped them to develop fulfilling relationships and rewarding careers and realize their dreams. It has allowed many individuals and families to prevent or relieve common ailments, as well as serious illnesses, and go on to lead active, healthy lives. Many doctors, nurses, and other health care professionals, including the late Benjamin Spock, MD, Christiane Northrup, MD, and Neal Barnard, MD, have observed this way of eating. Thousands of students have completed advanced training and become professional cooks, teachers, and dietary counselors. Macrobiotic menus and recipes have been incorporated into Ritz Carlton hotels, the Kellogg School of Management, Lemuel Shattack Hospital, and other businesses, schools, restaurants, hospitals, prisons, and religious and spiritual centers worldwide. Celebrated actors, musicians, and other artists—from Gloria Swanson and John Cage to John Lennon and Yoko Ono, from John Denver and Madonna to Sting and Alicia Silverstone—have engaged personal macrobiotic chefs because they know their food keeps them trim and fit, stabilizes their mind and emotions, and optimizes their performance.

We were fortunate to study and work with Michio for many years and manage, teach, and cook at Kushi Institute, the school the Kushis founded in the Berkshires. *The One Peaceful World Cookbook* is based on principles of whole-foods macrobiotic cooking that contribute to physical health and vitality, mental and emotional harmony, and spiritual well-being. The recipes in this book include centering whole grains, mineral-rich vegetables from land and sea, fiber-rich beans and bean products (e.g., tofu and tempeh), delectable fruits, seeds, nuts, strengthening fermented foods (e.g., miso, shoyu, and sauerkraut), and other natural products of the earth. The hundred and fifty plus tasty, easy-to-follow recipes in this book are based on the most recent macrobiotic dietary guidelines; scientific and medical studies documenting the personal and planetary health benefits of a balanced plant-based approach; and other cutting-edge research on nutrition and fitness.

In addition to practical material on holistic principles, how to set up your kitchen, and the recipes, this book includes concise introductory information on ki energy (or the life force that animates all living things), yin and yang (the complementary opposite energies of the universe), preparation tips, lifestyle guidance, medicinal drinks, and other home cares.

Macrobiotic cuisine is synonymous with delicious, healthy food, and for more than fifty years, the macrobiotic community has set the gold standard for balanced vegan cooking in the United States and around the world. *The One Peaceful World Cookbook* offers techniques on how to create balanced whole-food meals the entire family will enjoy. Its recipes reflect the diversity and ricÚess of the planet's cultures and culinary traditions: American (including dishes from the Northeast, Midwest, South, Southwest, West, and other regions), European (England, Wales, France, Germany, Italy, Russia), Asian (Japan, China, Korea, India, Indonesia, Vietnam), Central and South American (Mexico, Venezuela, Peru), African (Ghana, Ethiopia, Morocco), and the Middle East (Israel, Palestine).

THE MACROBIOTIC APPROACH

"The significance of macrobiotics in American life is little understood although it relates to such broad historical issues as the postwar move toward a more healthy diet, our increasingly global culture, alternative healing, peace studies, and traditions of grassroots activism."

—SMITHSONIAN INSTITUTION

From a tiny seed in the 1960s, macrobiotic teachings have blossomed, nourishing society at many levels. In the early 1970s, research on the macrobiotic community from Harvard University and the Framingham Heart Study identified dietary cholesterol and saturated fat as major risk factors in the development of heart disease. The scientists also found that individuals observing a macrobiotic way of eating (on average for two years) had the healthiest blood values of any group observed in modern society.

The landmark dietary and nutritional changes over the last several decades have been influenced and shaped by macrobiotics, from the historic *Dietary Goals* report by the Select Committee on Nutrition and Human Needs in the late 1970s to the US government's Food Guide Pyramid in the 1990s, from the creation of the Office of Alternative Medicine within the National Institutes of Health in the 1990s to the shift toward a plant-based diet and sustainable food and agricultural practices in the 2000s. As the new century began, the Smithsonian Institution honored the Kushis by establishing a permanent collection on macrobiotics at the National Museum of American History in Washington, DC, and exhibited Aveline Kushi's pressure cooker under the same roof as Ben Franklin's kite, the Gettysburg Address, and other national treasures.

These major changes constitute a nutritional axis shift. The Basic Four food groups of the mid-twentieth century—based on meat and dairy foods—were replaced with a more balanced way of eating centered on grains, vegetables, fruits, and other plant foods. As the twenty-first century began, the US Dietary Guidelines accompanying the Food Guide Pyramid called upon Americans to "use plant foods as the foundation of your meals":

> There are many ways to create a healthy eating pattern, but they all start with the three food groups at the base of the Pyramid: grains, fruits, and vegetables. Eating a variety of grains (especially whole grain foods), fruits, and vegetables is the basis of healthy eating. Enjoy meals that have rice, pasta, tortillas, or whole grain bread as the center of the plate . . . Eating plenty of whole grains, such as whole grain bread or oatmeal, as part of the healthful eating patterns described by these guidelines, may help protect you against many chronic diseases.[1]

---

[1] *Nutrition and Your Health: Dietary Guidelines for Americans*, Fifth ed. (Washington, DC: USDA and DHHS, 2000.)

The benefits of a macrobiotic way of eating have been recognized by the major scientific and medical societies and published in leading journals, including the *New England Journal of Medicine*, *Journal of the American Medical Association*, *American Journal of Clinical Nutrition*, and *Lancet*. Medical researchers at the University of Memphis and University of South Carolina recently evaluated the dietary pattern at Kushi Institute's flagship Way to Health program and concluded that it had a lower percentage of potentially harmful fats, higher total dietary fiber, and higher amounts of most micronutrients, including beta-carotene, B vitamins, and iron, than the standard American diet. "Findings from this analysis of a macrobiotic diet plan indicate the potential for disease prevention and suggest the need for studies of real-world consumption as well as designing, implementing, and testing interventions based on the macrobiotic approach," the scientists concluded in a 2015 article in the journal *Nutrition and Cancer*. Researchers at Tufts University and Columbia University are currently developing a macrobiotic intervention study for women with end-stage breast cancer. It is designed to be the first randomized clinical trial of its kind and could change the treatment paradigm for women worldwide.

In the macrobiotic community, we strive to live according to the spirit of "one grain, ten thousand grains." This timeless proverb points to the truth that nature is endlessly abundant. A single seed of rice yields a whole rice field. From an acorn, an entire forest grows. An apple contains a boundless number of orchards. Heirloom seeds—the traditional Staff of Life—that sustained and nourished humanity over the millennia were given to us at no cost. This law teaches us to be eternally grateful for the gifts of nature and to return or give away freely our understanding of health, life, and peace. Each thought, word, and deed produces visible and invisible effects that multiply endlessly. This is the natural order of the infinite universe.

Whether you are an experienced cook or a newcomer to the macrobiotic way, we hope that you will enjoy this cookbook and integrate some of its treasures into your daily life. It is a cardinal principle that people who eat healthful food together develop a common mind and spirit. They can intuitively understand and relate harmoniously with one another.

The recipes that follow offer an opportunity to share nature's bounty in the meals that you prepare. These delightful culinary gifts extend the chain of giving from the planet to you, and multiply the blessings of health and peace to all those around your dining table.

—Alex Jack and Sachi Kato

THE ART OF MACROBIOTIC COOKING

A JOYOUS, PEACEFUL WAY OF EATING

Ki refers to the natural electromagnetic energy of heaven and earth that manifests in all things. It is also called life energy, cosmic energy, or the vital force. In human beings, ki flows through the meridians, chakras, organs, tissues, and cells and carries vitality and consciousness. In China it is known as qi, in India as *prana*, in Judaism as *ruach*, in Christianity as the Holy Spirit, in Islam as *baraka*, and in Jungian psychology as synchronicity.

In the Far East, the ideogram for ki is made of characters for the steam or energy arising from cooking millet, rice, or other grain. The word for "health" in Japanese is *genki*—good ki. Originally, it was known that good or strong ki energy arose from eating a plant-based diet centered on cooked whole cereal grains. Sickness or bad ki—known as *byoki*—results from poor cooking and imbalanced eating. Our daily foods create our minds, bodies, and spirits. Through the art of cooking and proper eating, we distill and absorb the condensed energy and vibration of heaven and earth. Our life becomes joyful and naturally unfolds in harmony with nature and the cosmos.

Another fundamental concept is *wa*, the word for peace and harmony. It consists of the ideograms for "grain" and "mouth." Ancient people knew that eating brown rice, millet, or other whole grains as the principal food led to day-to-day good physical health and vitality; a calm, clear mind; and sound judgment. A grain-centered diet formed the foundation of a long, happy life.

In the West, the same principles are enshrined in Isaiah's admonition to beat swords into plowshares. The ancient Hebrew prophet knew that the secret of a just, enduring peace was to turn weapons of war into peaceful farming implements to grow grains, vegetables, and other crops. In the *Odyssey*, the Greek poet Homer relates how Odysseus' long journey home will finally end when he transforms his battle oar into a winnowing shovel—a tool to thresh barley and wheat. In the New Testament, the Lord's Prayer prevails on God to "give us this day our daily bread" and bless us to avoid temptations (extremes of yin and yang) and forgive others.

In our own era, the government's Food Guide Pyramid and MyPlate—with whole grains, fresh vegetables and fruit, and other plant foods as the foundation of a healthful diet—replaced the Basic Four food groups consisting of 50 percent meat, poultry, and dairy food. Over the last several decades, the rates of heart disease, cancer, and other chronic diseases have fallen following this nutritional axis shift. In the twenty-first century, a healthy, plant-based way of eating is rapidly spreading worldwide. The United Nations warns that the modern food and agriculture system, especially cattle production, is the main cause of global warming, loss of biodiversity, air and water pollution, and other environmental destruction. It is clear that animal-foods consumption today, even if organic quality, is unsustainable.

The key to health, happiness, and peace is preparing balanced, artistic meals from high quality and whole or traditionally processed foods. Food is not only energy; it is also spirit. Cooking with gratitude, consciously putting our love and energy in the food we cook, and blessing the meal to the health of our family, community, or planet is one of the most important aspects of the art of cooking. These considerations do not usually appear on the ingredient lists or step-by-step instructions in a cookbook. But for optimal health, vitality, and the realization of our common dream in life, they are essential. In these pages, we will offer inspiring quotes and tecÚiques to enhance the power, energy, and beauty of the food you prepare; nourish your heart and soul; and create joyous harmony and balance.

THE SEVEN QUALITIES OF MACROBIOTIC COOKING

1. **Natural** means whole food or unrefined food; for example, brown rice is preferred to white rice or whole wheat instead of white flour. Whole natural foods retain the full energy (ki, chi, or *prana*) of the crop and are ideal for optimal daily health and vitality. They are also higher in nutrients, antioxidants, and other health-giving compounds. For example, whole-grain rice or whole wheat retains from 50 to 100 percent more complex carbohydrates, fiber, vitamins, minerals, and trace elements than refined grains.

2. **Organic** foods are grown without chemical fertilizers, herbicides, pesticides, or other artificial sprays. Nor do they contain preservatives, colorings, other artificial ingredients, GMOs, growth hormones, or vaccines.

3. **Seasonal** signifies that for the most part we eat foods in the season they are grown, harvested, or stored. For example, fresh fruits retain optimal energy in late spring, summer, or early fall; sprouts, radishes, cucumbers, and other garden veggies in spring and summer; squashes and pumpkins in fall and winter; and grains, beans, and sea vegetables throughout the year.

4. **Ecological** eating respects the climate and environment in which foods are grown. For example, in the United States, which is mostly a four-season climate, the more healthful fruits to eat are apples, pears, peaches, berries, melons, and other temperate fruits rather than pineapples, mangoes, and other tropical fare. (These larger, juicier fruits, however, are suitable in warmer latitudes.) Practically speaking, foods that grow in an east or west direction are suitable for regular use, including produce from California if we live on the East Coast or from Europe, Russia, China, and Japan, places that share a similar climate. Eating foods that grow significantly north or south from where we live violates natural climactic and environmental boundaries and may lead to imbalances and an inability to adapt to our surroundings. Hence, in temperate regions we avoid or minimize hot spices (from the tropics) or heavy meat and dairy foods

(from the cold North, high mountains, or desert regions). However, in their native locales, these can be considered part of a traditional or macrobiotic way of eating.

5. **Unprocessed foods** are stronger and more vitalizing than processed foods. For example, whole oats give strong, warming energy, while steel-cut oats that have been mechanically cut into quarters or smaller pieces retain less ki energy and are not as hardy, as their strong, whole energy begins to disperse. Rolled oats or oat flakes that have been further reduced and cook up even more quickly contain the least amount of energy and vitality. All types of oats may be part of a balanced macrobiotic way of eating. For the most part, a majority of our grains and other foods should be in whole form and a smaller portion naturally processed. **Naturally processed** foods also include tofu, tempeh, miso, shoyu, and other traditionally made soy foods, as well as pickles, natural sweeteners, condiments, seasonings, and beverages that have been fermented or traditionally or minimally processed. These foods are an important part of the macrobiotic way of eating as long as they are made from the highest quality ingredients, aged naturally, and processed to avoid high temperatures, pressures, and other artificial or extreme conditions. They give a totally different energy than textured soy protein, soy meat substitutes, and other highly processed foods.

6. **Locally grown** foods that grow in our own area are generally fresher and more balanced than those that originate from across the country or around the globe. They also require less transportation, packaging, and distribution and are gentler on the earth. Growing your own food in a backyard organic garden is ideal. Next best is obtaining locally grown food from farmers' markets or CSA—Community Supported Agriculture—or purchasing shares of produce from local farms.

7. **Sustainable** foods benefit the planet as a whole, including the water, the air, the valleys and mountains, the plants, and human beings and other animals. Besides cattle plantations, giant agribusiness companies today are producing organic soybeans, maize, palm oil, and other monocultures that are threatening rainforests in South America, Southeast Asia, and elsewhere and are contributing to global warming and the loss of diversity. Similarly, the demand for quinoa, the traditional grain of the ancient Incans, in modern society has driven up prices and made it unaffordable to native Peruvians and Bolivians. Such foods are unsustainable. Fortunately, quinoa is now being grown in California and can be used instead of the Andean variety.

FIVE ESSENTIAL ELEMENTS

When properly cooked or prepared, macrobiotic-quality foods share five further qualities. They are fresh, tasty and delicious, beautiful, balanced, and full of ki.

1. **Fresh** food includes grains, beans, veggies, fruits, seeds, and nuts just harvested from the garden or brought to market, or naturally processed products such as tofu and

tempeh freshly made at home or purchased as soon as available. In the macrobiotic kitchen, industrially mass-produced foods, such as instant foods, sprayed foods, dyed foods, irradiated foods, genetically engineered foods, and chemically grown or treated foods, are avoided.

2. **Tasty and delicious** is not a phrase synonymous with most health foods. On the contrary, health foods have a reputation for being bland and tasteless. Macrobiotic cooking is widely appreciated for its exquisite flavor, taste, and texture. Because macrobiotics is based on principles of balance and harmony, food prepared this way quenches the appetite, delights the palate, and leaves one with a feeling of deep satisfaction and contentment. Of course, the art of macrobiotic cooking takes time to learn and master. But whether you are a beginner or an experienced chef, you will soon start preparing food that your entire family, friends, and colleagues will truly enjoy.

3. **Beautiful** food adds another layer of sensory enjoyment, aesthetic satisfaction, and spiritual serenity to the meal. In the macrobiotic community, we stress the art of plating and strive to make each dish or meal an artistic masterpiece. Garnishes, sauces and dressings, and other special toppings, fillings, and touches enhance the beauty of the meal. Special plates, bowls, serving dishes, utensils,

napkins, and other cookware featuring natural colors and textures further accentuate the dining experience. Finally, flowers, leaves, pinecones, gourds, seashells, or other seasonal flourishes at the table make a macrobiotic meal a memorable experience.

4. **Balanced** food consciously blends principles of balance and harmony to create a meal that is greater than the sum of its parts. Ideally, each meal is based on humanity's traditional way of eating, the climate and environment, the season and weather, and the sex, age, and personal health, vitality, and needs of everyone at the table. For example, at the start of a meal, miso, a fermented soybean product with living enzymes, is frequently used to make soup that replicates the ancient ocean in which primitive life began. Today, wild grains and grasses, the traditional staples of humanity, are consumed largely in the form of cultivated whole grains, noodles and pasta, and other grain products such as bread, seitan, and fu. Sea vegetables offer a subtle, unique energy from the ancient sea that balances vegetables, fruits, seeds and nuts, and more recent plant life that evolved on land. By consuming foods from land and sea, mountain and plain, above and below

ground, we take in the entire spiral of life on our planet and develop a comprehensive mind and universal spirit.

5. **Life energy** (ki) flows naturally between heaven and earth. All living things radiate natural electromagnetic energy. This energy is especially concentrated in seeds. Whole unhulled rice, for example, naturally retains its ki energy for years—centuries and millennia, in some cases—and like other whole cereal grains is a principal food for longevity. Beans, seeds and nuts, and sea vegetables also retain their vitality over time. Ancient lotus root seeds dating to fifteen hundred years ago recently propagated and gave birth to strong, healthy new offspring. Of course, a balanced macrobiotic meal might also include leafy greens, delicate soups, quick crispy vegetables, fresh fruit, and other light, fresh foods to balance the strong life force in the hardy grains, beans, and other seeds that are the foundation of a long, happy life.

   Ki energy can be further enhanced through special farming and gardening tecÚiques, cooking methods, artfully designed cookware, serene music, grace at meals, prayer, meditation, chanting, and other spiritual practices. Unfortunately, most modern food, especially fast food and artificial food, has little or no ki. As a result, the nutrients in food have steadily declined in recent decades. The use of new high-yielding hybrid seeds and marketing methods that emphasize shelf life over fresÚess have weakened most industrially grown and artificially processed food. As much as possible, foods should be made with heirloom, open-pollinated, standard or nonhybrid seeds that retain the life force and vitality of the original variety.

YIN AND YANG

In our classes, students are taught to cook using the compass of yin and yang. Yin and yang are the complementary opposite energies that flow between heaven and earth and make up all things.

Yang refers to the energy of the cosmos spiraling centripetally toward the earth. It is a contracting force and is more downward, inward, heavy, dense, material, and physical. Yin is the energy of the earth that spirals toward the heavens in an opposite, centrifugal direction. It is an expanding force and is more upward, outward, light, mental, psychological, and spiritual in orientation.

Nothing is exclusively yin or yang. Everything combines these elemental energies, and their proportion changes. As a rule, males are slightly more yang, females slightly more yin, but both sexes are constantly nourished by the streaming energies of heaven and earth.

In respect to diet, our principal food—whole grains—is more yang, or condensed, while vegetables, the next largest food group, is more yin, or expanded. The next most consumed foods—beans and sea vegetables—are also more on the yang side, while fruits, oil, seeds, nuts, and beverages are more yin. Within each category, foods can be further classified according to their relative qualities. Compared to barley and oats, millet and quinoa are yang.

Compared to carrots and daikon radish, collards and other leafy greens are more yin. Together these daily foods are prepared with salt (very yang) and water (very yin) and a variety of other seasonings, condiments, and garnishes to create a balanced meal. Altogether these foods can be classified as moderate and occupy the center of the food spectrum between extremes. They help us maintain optimal health, a calm, clear mind, and sound judgment. As plant-based foods, they are also beneficial for the planet.

YIN AND YANG FACTORS IN FOOD SELECTION AND PREPARATION

QUALITIES	MORE YANG	MORE YIN
TASTE	salty, bitter, umami, or mildly sweet	sour, pungent, or strongly sweet
SMELL	less odor or aroma	stronger odor or aroma
TEXTURE	harder, thicker, drier, crunchier	softer, thinner, moister, smoother, creamier
COOKING METHODS	pressure-cooking, long-time boiling, broiling, baking, pan-frying, tempura or deep-frying, long fermenting	raw or uncooked, steaming, low or medium boiling, quick sautéing, pressing, short fermenting
TIME	longer cooking	shorter cooking
VOLUME	smaller serving	larger serving
ENVIRONMENT	colder, more temperate	warmer, more tropical
SEASON	autumn and winter	spring and summer
SOIL	drier and more volcanic	more watery and sedimentary
GROWING DIRECTION	vertically growing downward; expanding horizontally above the ground	vertically growing upward; expanding horizontally underground
GROWING SPEED	growing slower	growing faster
SIZE	smaller, more compact	larger, more expanded
HEIGHT	shorter	taller
WATER CONTENT	drier	juicier and more watery
COLOR	yellow, brown, beige, orange, red	green, blue, violet
CHEMICAL COMPONENTS	less potassium and other yin elements; more sodium and other yang elements	more potassium and other yin elements; less sodium and other yang elements
NUTRITION	more carbohydrate and minerals	more fat and protein

continued on next page . . .

QUALITIES	MORE YANG	MORE YIN
PARTS OF THE PLANT	roots, seeds	leaves, stems, flowers, fruits
GRAINS	smaller, rounder, and growing in a colder climate	larger, longer, and growing in a warmer climate
BEANS	smaller	larger
VEGETABLES	root and round	leafy green or white
FRUIT	smaller, growing on the ground, or in a colder climate	larger, growing in trees, or in a warmer climate
SEEDS	smaller	larger
NUTS	smaller, less oily	larger, more oily
SEASONING	more salt, miso, or shoyu; less oil, vinegar, herbs, or spices	less salt, miso, shoyu; more oil, vinegar, herbs, or spices
BEVERAGES	warmer, nonaromatic, or nonstimulating	colder, aromatic, or stimulating

TYPES OF COOKING

There are five general types of cooking:

1. **Cooking for Daily Health and Vitality.** Day-to-day food is tasty, delicious, and energizing. It gives a calm, clear mind, sound judgment, and optimal vitality. Within this category, foods may be classified as appropriate for daily *regular use*, four or five times a week; foods for *occasional use*, one to three times a week; foods for *infrequent use*, once or twice a month; and foods to *avoid or minimize* because they are inappropriate for our climate and environment, condition of health, or personal needs. In temperate regions, the latter includes meat, poultry, eggs, fatty fish, dairy food, refined grains; yeasted breads and baked goods; nightshade plants (tomato, potato, eggplant, tobacco); sugar and other refined simple sugars; and stimulants (coffee, chocolate, strong herbs and hot spices, and hard alcohol).
2. **Cooking for Enjoyment and Celebration.** On holidays and festive occasions, we enjoy richer, more elaborate food, including a wider variety of tastes, flavors, spices and herbs, and other ingredients. Special or party food is an important part of a natural, healthy way of life.
3. **Cooking for Healing and Recovery.** If we are tired, low energy, or ill and ailing, we may need to eat a simpler, more basic diet. We may need to avoid or minimize oil, salt, and other seasonings, fruit, salad, sweets, or bread and baked goods. Generally, after

several days, weeks, or months, depending on the mildness or severity of the condition, the diet can be widened out and the restricted items gradually increased. There are also a variety of medicinal drinks, special dishes, and compresses, poultices, and other external applications for conditions ranging from colds and headaches to high blood pressure and hardening of the arteries, to diabetes, arthritis, cancer, and other chronic diseases. For the most part, these home remedies are made from ordinary, everyday foods and do not require any special knowledge or a specialist to prescribe or prepare.

4. **Cooking for Personal Development and Realizing Our Dream.** Once we have discovered our dream in life, we may tailor our daily way of eating to achieving our goals. For example, a competitive athlete, professional dancer, or farmer will usually need more energizing and activating foods than a writer, artist, or teacher, who will need more uplifting and relaxing menus and recipes. A male will generally need stronger, more dynamic food than a female and also the quantity may be slightly larger. A girl or woman, on the other hand, may require more fruits, salads, and sweets than a boy or man. A baby or young child will crave a more natural sweet taste than an older child or adult. An adult of middle age will generally consume more food than an elder. An older person usually requires more oil than a younger person. As our health is enhanced, we discover our dream in life and then eat accordingly to manifest and realize that larger goal or purpose.

5. **Cooking for Spiritual Development.** To refine our mind and spirit and deepen our understanding of life, strong, nourishing daily fare is essential, including a balanced diet of whole grains, beans, vegetables, and sea vegetables. From time to time, for greater spiritual insights or better practice, a very simple way of eating may be followed for several days or more. This may consist of a meal with just a bowl of grain, a cup of miso or other simple soup, a few pickles or slices of cooked vegetables, and a cup of bancha twig tea. Chewing thoroughly is a cardinal macrobiotic practice to develop our intuition and understanding, as well as to strengthen our physical health and vitality. Eating to only about 80 percent of capacity is also recommended to keep open the channel of energy connecting us with heaven and earth. If we eat to capacity or overeat, the central energy channel charging our meridians, chakras, organs, systems, and functions can become blocked and dull, and the energy will not flow freely.

MEAL OPTIONS

For those sensitive to gluten, we offer gluten-free options, including tamari (a soy sauce made without wheat) instead of shoyu (which contains wheat) and entrées using rice, millet, or quinoa instead of wheat, barley, or rye.

In some macrobiotic households, white-meat fish is served once or twice a week for those who eat animal foods, and they might find that it gives them a burst of strong, dynamic energy.

It is considered optional. Over the years, the number of people in the macrobiotic community who eat fish and seafood has steadily decreased. In a world of rapid climate change, marine life is increasingly polluted and unsustainable, and vegan macrobiotic cuisine has become the norm. This book completely avoids the use of animal-based food.

CONTAINS GLUTEN	GLUTEN-FREE
wheat (including wheat berries, flour, and bread), kamut, couscous, bulgur, seitan, fu, other wheat products	brown rice (including brown rice flour and bread), sweet rice, basmati rice, wild rice, mochi, and other rice products
soba noodles (40% buckwheat / 60% wheat), ramen, spaghetti, linguini, and other wheat or spelt varieties	soba noodles (100% buckwheat), noodles and pasta made from brown rice, millet, quinoa, mung bean, azuki bean, sweet potato, kuzu, and other gluten-free varieties
barley	millet
spelt	oats (oats have to be certified gluten-free)
rye	quinoa, amaranth, buckwheat, teff
barley miso	brown rice miso, chickpea miso, hatcho miso
shoyu	tamari
barley malt	brown rice syrup, maple syrup
beer	sake

PRINCIPLES OF COOKING

Macrobiotic cooking is unique. Natural and simple ingredients are best for creating delicious food that is nourishing, tasty, and attractive. The cook has the ability to change the quality of the food. Stronger cooking—using greater pressure, salt, heat, and time—makes the energy of the food more concentrated (creating a more yang effect). Lighter cooking—using less pressure, salt, heat, and time—produces a lighter energy (more yin). A good cook manages these energies according to the needs of those she or he cooks for. In this way, the cook influences and shapes the health, consciousness, and well-being of her family or household. Harmony and balance can be created by varying the following aspects in our day-to-day food preparation:

- Our daily meals should consist primarily of cereal grains and grain products (theme) complemented with a variety of vegetables, beans, sea vegetables, fruits, seeds and nuts, and other predominantly plant-based foods (variation).

- The methods of cooking, such as style (e.g., blanching, sautéing, stewing, pressure-cooking), use of higher or lower flame, length of cooking time, and source and amount of water used, should be varied.
- Various styles of cutting should be used. When cutting food materials, it is preferable that each piece should reflect both yin and yang qualities, an art taught in macrobiotic cooking classes.
- It is best to use as much of each vegetable as possible. For example, cook root veggies without peeling off their skins, and cook their tops as greens.
- Before cooking, chopped food materials are ideally kept separate—not mixed—to avoid premature interchange of quality.
- The best source of energy for cooking in today's modern world is natural gas, followed by wood and charcoal. Solar or other renewable natural energy sources for cooking are on the horizon and should be encouraged.
- The best quality of water for drinking and cooking is spring water, well water, or mountain stream water. Chemically treated municipal water, as well as distilled water, is preferably avoided. In urban settings, filtered water is often the best alternative. Adjusting the amount of water used (and occasionally the source or quality) creates balance and variety.
- Sea salt is preferable to table salt, which lacks the many minerals and trace elements found in the ocean. Pure white sea salt that flows freely is preferable to gray, yellow, pink, or clumpy sea salt that is too high in sodium and other minerals. The taste of seasoning should not be overpowering but only used to bring out and enhance the natural taste of the food itself. Vary the type and amount of seasoning used frequently.
- The length of cooking time should be varied. For example, along with soup and salad, a main meal will typically include a long-cooked grain dish; a root vegetable, sea vegetable, or sweet round vegetable dish that takes a moderate time to cook; and a quick, crispy vegetable dish that cooks up in several minutes.
- After cooking, food begins to lose its ki energy, so it should be eaten as soon as possible. As a rule, prepare the main whole grain fresh every day and eat it up over the next twenty-four hours. Miso soup, leafy greens, and other light, delicate dishes should also be made fresh each meal. Beans, round and root veggies, thick soups, sea veggies, and other hardier, long-cooked dishes will keep in the refrigerator for two to three days.

The way of eating is as important as the food itself. Meals should be kept peaceful and relaxed. Try to eat at regular times two or three times a day. A quiet, soothing environment (free of TV, the Internet, and other artificial electromagnetic stimulation) is also recommended.

Methods of Cooking and Food Preparation

The following methods of cooking and food preparation are used in macrobiotic cooking according to the following guidelines:

Regular Use (daily or often)	Occasional Use	Special Occasions
blanching	pressure-cooking	grilling
boiling	wok-frying	smoked
steaming	deep-frying	frozen
waterless (nishime)	tempura	
soup	broiling	
sautéing (with oil or water)	baking	
pickling	roasting	
pressing/marinating		
fresh/raw		

STANDARD MACROBIOTIC WAY OF EATING

The standard macrobiotic way of eating is not a fixed or rigid diet but a set of flexible dietary principles that can be adjusted or modified according to climate and environment, season and weather, sex and age, activity level and condition of health, and enjoyment and personal needs. In temperate regions, the standard approach for people in general good health consists of the following food categories:

Whole cereal grains and grain products make up about 40 to 50 percent of our daily food by total weight of food consumed each day (this comes to about one-quarter to one-third by volume of a plate at each meal). Whole grains include brown rice, whole wheat, millet, barley, maize, and quinoa. Grains may also be eaten in the form of noodles or pasta, either Eastern-style (e.g., udon, soba, *somen*) or Western-style (e.g., spaghetti, spirals, shells), especially if the flour is whole grain and not refined or polished. Noodles and other unbaked flour products, such as pancakes, crepes, tortillas, and chapatis, are more digestible than hard baked flour products. In small volume, however, bread and other baked goods, especially sourdough wheat, spelt, or rye, may be consumed a few times a week. Grain products such as rice cakes, puffed cereals, crackers, and other grain products are dry and contracting, so are best eaten less often.

Soup, consisting of one or two cups a day. Soup broth made with miso, to which land and sea vegetables are added, is prepared frequently. Soups made with grains, beans, and vegetables are also often served.

Vegetable dishes make up about 25 to 30 percent of daily food and include fresh (and occasionally dried) veggies cooked in a variety of ways, as mentioned above. Salads are enjoyed pressed, blanched, or fresh. Root vegetables such as carrots, daikon, turnips, lotus root, rutabaga are eaten regularly. Collards, kale, mustard greens, bok choy, broccoli, and other green leafy veggies are steamed, blanched, or sautéed and enjoyed one to three times a day. Sweet vegetables including winter squash, onions, and cabbage are also enjoyed daily. In general, about two-thirds of the vegetables are cooked and up to one-third raw.

Beans, green protein, and sea vegetables make up another 5 to 10 percent of daily food intake. Beans for regular use include lentils, chickpeas, azuki beans, and black soybeans. Other beans such as split peas, pinto beans, kidney beans, and navy beans may also be used frequently. Soy products such as tofu, tempeh, and *natto* may be used regularly in moderation and served as the main protein of the meal. Other types of green protein such as seitan (wheat gluten marinated with shoyu) and fu (unseasoned wheat gluten) are also enjoyed on occasion. Nori sheets and wakame are used daily in soups. A small strip of kombu is used for cooking grains and beans, while arame, hijiki, and other strong sea vegetables are enjoyed a couple of times a week as a side dish.

Fruit, seeds, and nuts are consumed several times a week as a snack or added to special dishes or as dessert, ideally during the season they are grown. In temperate zones, preferred fruits include apples, strawberries, cherries, plums, apricots, and melons, and less often tangerines, oranges, and grapefruit. Fruit juice is highly concentrated and its use should be moderate. Fruit is enjoyed fresh, dried, and cooked with a pinch of sea salt to bring out its sweetness. Almonds, walnuts, pecans, and other temperate nuts are preferred to macadamia, cashew, Brazil, and other tropical varieties.

Salt, oil, and other seasonings are key ingredients in macrobiotic cooking. For daily use, unrefined sesame oil (especially light sesame) or olive oil are used in moderation. Other unrefined plant oils, such as dark or toasted sesame, safflower, or sunflower oil, are used on occasion, but saturated or hydrogenated oils are avoided. Canola is also avoided because it is primarily an industrial oil. Naturally processed sea salt, nonchemicalized miso and shoyu, and tamari may be used as seasonings. Daily meals, however, should not have an overly salty flavor, and as a rule seasonings are used in cooking and not added at the table.

Other regular seasonings include ginger, lemon, lime, rice vinegar, umeboshi vinegar, and umeboshi plum or paste.

Pickles, especially homemade varieties, are eaten daily in small volume to aid in digesting grains and vegetables. They may be made with various root and round vegetables preserved in sea salt, rice bran, shoyu, umeboshi, or miso. Short-time, less salty pickles are enjoyed in warmer weather, while long-time, saltier ones are eaten in colder seasons.

Condiments are optional foods that are available on the table to supply a special taste, color, or energy. They allow family members to individually adjust taste and seasoning. Condiments for regular use include *gomashio* (sesame seed salt), roasted seaweed powders, umeboshi plums, shiso powder, and green nori flakes.

Garnishes are used to balance dishes at the table and beautify the meal. Regular garnishes include chopped scallions, parsley, alfalfa and other sprouts, grated ginger, grated daikon, grated radish, lemon or other citrus slices, horseradish, and wasabi.

Snacks and desserts are enjoyed in moderation. Snacks include seeds and nuts (about one-quarter to one-half cup once or more times a week), especially pumpkin seeds, sunflower seeds, almonds, walnuts, pecans, mochi, hummus, popcorn, and rice cakes. Desserts are enjoyed several times a week and include kanten, cake, stewed fruits, and other sweet dishes prepared with natural ingredients. Naturally sweet ingredients such as apples, fall and winter squash, pumpkin, and dried fruit are favored. Grain-based natural sweeteners such as brown rice syrup, barley malt, and *amazake* (a cultured rice beverage) are used for a more concentrated sweet taste. Chestnuts, dried fruit, apple juice, and occasionally maple syrup are also enjoyed in small volume.

Beverages for daily use include *bancha* twig tea (also known as *kukicha*), roasted barley tea, other grain-based drinks, and other nonaromatic, nonstimulant teas as well as water. For occasional use, amazake, grain coffee, green tea, and fruit or vegetable juice or cider are enjoyed. Fruit-sweetened spritzers, beer, sake, and other mild alcoholic beverages are reserved for special occasions.

GENERAL HEALTH AND ENVIRONMENTAL GUIDELINES FOR COOKWARE AND EATING UTENSILS

Generally avoided:

- Most exotic and rare woods
- Aluminum, except when used as a cover that does not come in contact with food
- Nonrecyclable plastics and packaging
- Treated nonstick pans and cookware

- Copper
- Products containing lead or other heavy metals and toxins
- Disposable products

Universally approved:
- Bamboo with nontoxic finishes
- Common woods with nontoxic finishes
- Stainless steel
- Cast iron
- No-lead earthenware
- No-lead ceramics
- Recycled glass
- Unbleached and vegetable-dyed organic cotton products
- 100 percent recycled unbleached paper products with at least 15 percent postconsumer waste

COOKING FOR KI ENERGY AND VITALITY

In addition to food quality, the way we cook contributes to our energy, vitality, and balance. The quick, relaxing energy of blanching, steaming, and stir-frying vegetables balances stewing or pressure-cooking of grains and beans that give a slow, heavier, more grounding energy.

Blanching and steaming are central ways of preparing vegetables. These cooking styles give active energy and fresÚess. Quick cooking preserves their natural energy and texture, brightens their color, and brings out the natural taste in the food. Overcooking vegetables makes for limp, tasteless, colorless vegetables.

Stewing is also frequently used in macrobiotic cooking for grains, beans, and vegetables from land and sea. During stewing, it is preferable to refrain from frequent mixing and stirring as much as possible, allowing foods to mix themselves and bring out their own natural energy and flavors. This style of cooking makes for a hearty, warming, calming dish.

Sautéing with a small amount of oil and water is a more active energetic way of cooking. For those on a milder or healing diet, a small amount of water instead of oil can be added to the skillet to water-sauté vegetables. Another method is pan-frying, in which the foods cook in the skillet for a moderate period of time with oil. Wok cooking calls for frequent stirring (and shaking of the entire pan) over a high flame. This gives strong, dynamic energy and balances the more moderate energy and vibration of other, slower, more long-cooked dishes.

Tempura, or deep-frying, gives strong, dynamic energy and a rich, satisfying taste. Baking creates foods that are evenly cooked with radiant heat, giving a deep warming energy and rich, delicious taste. Broiling, grilling, barbecuing, smoking, and other strong methods of cooking are reserved for parties and other special occasions.

The cooking flame also influences the energy of the dish and meal. A high flame or high heat gives stronger, more activating results. A medium flame or heat gives moderate, steady energy. A low flame or simmering heat gives a slower, more calming energy. For variety, all types of flame and heat may be used, with an emphasis on a moderate fire.

Blenders, food processors, toasters, and other electrical gadgets are avoided for medicinal cooking in the macrobiotic kitchen. They affect the quality of the food and give chaotic or dispersing energy. For medicinal cooking, a *suribachi* (Japanese mortar) and pestle, a Foley food mill (turned by hand), and other traditional implements are recommended. It is recommended not to use electric appliances; however, since we live in a busy modern world, mindful use of these appliances is called for in our recipes. We can neutralize the chaotic energy by simmering cooked foods or allowing food to rest before serving.

The Art of Chewing

"Chew, chew, chew your food,
Gaily through the meal,
The more you laugh, the less you eat,
The better you will feel."

—NURSERY RHYME

As this nursery rhyme reminds us, chewing is good for body and soul. It takes practice in today's fast-paced society for people to learn to chew properly or take time to digest their food. Both children and parents today gulp down their food on the go. They consume prepared and processed foods that are soft, lack fiber and texture, and require little if any effort to break down and digest.

Chewing's benefits include:

- Releasing saliva and activating ptyalin and other enzymes that are essential to breaking down food in the digestive organs, metabolizing it in the small intestine, and transporting it to the blood, where it nourishes our entire being
- Coating food with enzyme-rich saliva that protects against potentially harmful viruses, bacteria, and other microorganisms, as well as chemicals, radiation, and other toxins contained in the food
- Making grains and other foods sweeter to the taste, stimulating the appetite, and contributing to greater awareness of texture, smell, and aroma
- Helping stabilize the emotions and contributing to the aesthetic enjoyment of the meal by slowing down consumption and improving taste
- Improving digestion and assimilation, requiring less overall food to be consumed, thereby using less energy, reducing food waste (including less packaging materials, transport, and disposal), and contributing to a sustainable planet

For better health and well-being, as Gandhi, a marathon chewer, allegedly quipped, "Chew your liquids and drink your foods."

OBTAINING YOUR FOOD

In setting up your kitchen, it is essential to obtain the freshest and highest quality natural foods. Growing your own food is ideal, as is making your own tofu, miso, or seitan at home. For most people in modern society, the local natural foods stores such as co-op markets, farmers' markets, and CSA will be the primary sources of their daily food. Whole Foods Markets and other national chains and even ordinary supermarkets are increasingly selling organic and natural foods.

SETTING UP YOUR KITCHEN

Ideally, whole grains, noodles, flour, beans, sea vegetables, seeds and nuts, and other dry goods are bought in bulk or packages and stored in your kitchen. Large glass jars will help keep out moisture, bugs, and other spoilage or contamination.

Vegetables, fruit, and other fresh produce are best purchased several times a week so that they are consumed when fresh. When storing your produce, here are some tips to follow:

- Keep onions, sweet potatoes, and winter squashes in a cool, dry place, *not* in the refrigerator, and in a separate vessel from fruits.
- Store unripe fruits such as apples, pears, peaches, and avocados on the counter, moving them to the refrigerator if they begin to overripen.
- Citrus fruits may also be kept in a cool place for up to a week.
- If you obtain vegetables with leafy tops such as red radishes and turnips, separate the roots from the tops and store separately in the refrigerator.

The following is a suggested list of cookware you will need to have a fully stocked macrobiotic kitchen and be able to create delicious, healthy meals:

- A **natural gas range** gives a slow, steady, natural vibration and is ideal for daily cooking and medicinal preparations. For those without gas, a small two-burner camping stove that uses propane or other natural gas canisters may be used instead, especially for miso soup, the main grain of the day, and other principal dishes.
- A **pressure cooker** is beneficial for cooking whole grains and beans. It gives strong, peaceful energy; sweetens the taste of food; and saves on time and fuel. Stainless steel or enamel is recommended.
- **Cooking pots**, including a variety of saucepans, skillets, and other cookware, are essential. A well-seasoned wok is also recommended, especially for quick, high-energy stir-fries. Stainless steel and cast-iron are ideal; ceramic, enamelware, and heatproof glass cookware may also be used.

- A **flame deflector**, or heat diffuser, is a small circular device placed under a pressure cooker or pot to help distribute heat more evenly and prevent burning. Avoid asbestos pads.
- A **suribachi** is a Japanese-style ceramic bowl with grooves set into its beveled interior. It is used with a wooden pestle (called a *surikogi*) in preparing *gomashio* or other condiments, mashed foods, dressings, dips, and other items. A six-inch size is suitable for ordinary use but it is ideal to have several different sizes depending on the usage.
- A **flat grater** made of enamel, ceramic, or stainless steel is useful to grate fresh ginger, daikon, and other vegetables by hand.
- A **pickle press** is used to prepare pickles and pressed salads. A bowl or crock with a heavy weight or plate on top may also be used.
- A bamboo **steamer** or a folding stainless-steel steamer that fits inside a saucepan is used to steam or warm up foods.
- **Wire mesh strainers** and a colander are useful for washing grains, beans, sea vegetables, and other vegetables and for draining noodles. A fine mesh strainer is good for washing millet, quinoa, amaranth, sesame seeds, and smaller items, while a coarse one can handle rice, barley, and other larger grains. A flat strainer is helpful for removing blanched veggies from boiling water.

- A **vegetable knife** is essential for cutting. A sharp, high-quality knife with a wide rectangular blade or *Santoku* style knife enables vegetables to be cut evenly, quickly, and attractively. Stainless-steel and carbon-steel models are recommended.
- A **cutting board** for slicing vegetables should consist of a clean, flat surface. Wooden cutting boards are ideal, especially soft wood such as gingko and cedar, which are best for protecting vegetable knives from damage. The cutting board should be wiped clean after each use. If animal-based foods are prepared, a separate cutting board should be used to avoid contamination.
- A **hand food mill** is useful for puréeing soups, baby foods, and other dishes requiring a creamy texture. They are also used for medicinal preparations when electrical appliances are avoided.
- **Glass jars** are helpful to store grains, beans, seeds, nuts, shiitake mushrooms, and other foods.
- A **shoyu/tamari dispenser** is a small glass bottle with a spout and is useful to control the quantity of soy sauce used in cooking.
- A **tea kettle** made of glass or stainless steel is ideal for making *kukicha*, barley, or other tea. Small bamboo or wire mesh strainers are also recommended.

- A **vegetable brush** with natural bristles is useful for cleaning vegetables and a small **oil brush** is used to lightly coat a skillet.
- **Utensils** made of wood such as spoons, rice paddles, spatulas, and long cooking chopsticks are recommended since they will not scratch pots and pans or leave a metallic taste in the food. Wooden chopsticks, in addition to ordinary silverware, may also be used for eating. Avoid plastic and metal as much as possible.
- **Bamboo mats** are used to make sushi rolls. They are useful in covering cooked food. They are designed to allow heat to escape and air to enter so that food remains hot until served. You can also use them to protect bowls of grains and beans while they are soaking.
- **Cheesecloth** is made of 100 percent cotton and is useful for straining soft grains and some medicinal preparations, while **twine** is helpful for pickling and for selected medicinal applications.

Paleo vs. Macro

Paleo, a popular dietary trend, hearkens back to the Stone Age. According to its proponents, Paleolithic humans hunted mastodon, antelope, bison, and other large mammals, and meat constituted their major fare.

Present-day Paleos eat primarily grass-fed beef and other livestock, fish, eggs, cultured dairy, vegetables, fruit, roots, tubers, seeds, and nuts. For the most part, they avoid grains, potatoes, sugar, processed oils, and other domestically grown or processed fare. According to proponents, Paleolithic hunter-gatherers remained largely free of disease, and our species' decline can be traced to the advent of farming and grain consumption, which led to the onset of degenerative diseases.

In contrast to this theory, macrobiotics holds that cereal grains, evolved from wild grasses, constituted humanity's staple food. Recent archaeological discoveries support this view and demonstrate the primacy of whole grains to Paleolithic cultures. In East Africa, for example, scientists found evidence of extensive milling and baking of sorghum dating to one hundred thousand years ago. In multiple European sites, including present-day Moravia, Italy, and Russia, evidence has surfaced of ancient grain harvesting, cooking, and processing dating to about twenty-five thousand to thirty thousand years ago.

In another dramatic finding, researchers reported that "a new look at the diets of ancient African hominids shows a 'game change' occurred about 3.5 million years ago when some members added grasses or sedges to their menus" (*Proceedings of the National Academy of Sciences*, 2014). The change in diet to wild grasses, the progenitors of millet, rice, sorghum, and teff, and sedges like water chestnut, was "an important step in becoming human."

Boiled Rice
(see recipe on page 30)

PERFECT RICE

"Among cereal grains, brown rice is the most balanced. Its size, shape, color, texture, and proportion of carbohydrate, fat, protein, and minerals fall in the middle of the spectrum of the seven principal grains. Rice is biologically the most integrated grain— our evolutionary counterpart in the plant world."

—Aveline Kushi

THE POPULARITY OF BROWN RICE, THE ICONIC MACROBIOTIC FOOD, HAS SPREAD around the world. It is served in homes, schools, restaurants, hospitals, prisons, stadiums, and other institutions and venues. The medical profession has touted its benefits to prevent heart disease, cancer, diabetes, and other chronic diseases, and MyPlate recommends it as one of the whole grains to be eaten daily. NASA has even included brown rice in its menu for astronauts on the International Space Station.

High in nutrients, brown rice retains the bran, endosperm, fiber, and essential vitamins and minerals in the outer layers of the kernel that are removed in milling white rice. It is also high in ki energy and gives strong physical vitality, emotional equilibrium, and a calm, peaceful mind. Unlike wheat, barley, and other grains, rice does not have a line or crease in the middle. Its whole form and structure, representing the evolutionarily most advanced grain, further contributes to its spiritual vibration and energy and unifying qualities.

The most widely consumed food on the planet, rice has been a staple from time immemorial. It is hulled, milled, or processed into dozens of products, including sake, amazake, rice vinegar, rice cakes, and rice syrup, making it also the world's most versatile crop. The plant dates back to Pangaea, the primeval landmass that separated into two supercontinents. About twenty to thirty million years ago, northern and southern varieties of rice evolved separately in Asia and Africa. Until recently, wild rice in North America was considered an unrelated annual grass. But recent genetic research found that it is closely related to Asian rice, diverging from a common ancestor only about one million years ago.

Rice also has a rich cultural and social history. Prince Siddhartha ate rice under a tree and became the Buddha, or Enlightened One. Lao-tzu, Confucius, Ashoka, and Gandhi sang its praises. Leonardo da Vinci, Shakespeare, and Thomas Jefferson delighted in it. When he was ill, Charles Darwin recuperated on it. Rice has played a pivotal role in world history, serving as the principal food for many ancient civilizations. In the Middle Ages, it came to Europe over the fabled Silk Road and contributed to the flourishing of the Renaissance. Rice farming was widespread in West Africa, and rice influenced Spanish, French, Italian, and other Mediterranean cultures by way of Arabia and the Moors. In pre-Columbian America, native peoples enjoyed wild rice from the Great Lakes to Appalachia. In colonial times, rice was a key component of the economies of Virginia, the Carolinas, and Georgia, before it was displaced by cotton. The modern macrobiotic community popularized brown rice in the United States, Europe, and Japan, and it has now become a staple of planetary cuisine.

Rice retains its vitality almost indefinitely, and there are documented instances of rice sprouting after thousands of years. Several years ago, we experimented with rice propagated from seeds unearthed in an ancient tomb in Japan. This hardy, dry land rice comes in many hues and has strong, unifying energy. Dry land and paddy irrigation varieties are now being grown abundantly in the Northeast, Midwest, and other regions where rice has not been grown before.

Besides supporting personal health, rice contributes to planetary health and well-being. Rice fields constitute the single largest sanctuary for wildlife in the world. Hundreds of species of birds, mammals, insects, amphibians, reptiles, and little fish live in rice fields. In the Sacramento Valley of California, site of the most organic rice production in the country, one-quarter of all migrating geese, ducks, and other waterfowl set down in the rice fields to glean grains left from the harvest. Monarch butterflies, bees, and other threatened insects also thrive in rice fields.

RICE VARIETIES

Rice is classified into short, medium, and long grain. Short-grain rice is smaller, rounder, and hardier than the other varieties. It is the most popular type used in the modern macrobiotic community. Sweet brown rice is a glutinous type of short-grain rice used to make mochi and *ohagi*. Medium-grain rice is slightly softer, lighter, and less sweet than short-grain rice. It is traditionally used in warmer climates or seasons, makes delicious fried rice, and is used in Italian risotto and Spanish *arròs negre*. Long-grain rice is the staple in warmer regions and the tropics and cooks up lighter and fluffier than other varieties. Basmati rice is an aromatic type of long-grain rice from Pakistan and India, while jasmine rice, another fragrant variety, comes from Thailand, Vietnam, and other regions of Southeast Asia.

Most American macrobiotic households prepare organically grown short-grain or occa-sionally medium-grain rice, which can be combined with a long-grain rice such as basmati in warmer seasons. There are also several exotic rices that can be used from time to time, such as black rice and red rice. And while white rice is best avoided on a regular basis, now and then it makes for a nice, light accompaniment to the meal.

Organic rice is now widely available in natural foods stores and in many supermarkets. It is best stored in closed glass jars to prevent infestation by insects or rodents. Rice is also susceptible to going bad at high temperatures; therefore, store rice in a dark, cool place.

WASHING AND SOAKING RICE

The first step in cooking rice is to remove any small stones, dirt, damaged pieces, or other impurities. Place the grain in a bowl and cover with cold water until about an inch of liquid remains on top. With your fingers, gently stir the rice and then pour off the water. Repeat one or two more times and then transfer the rice, a handful at a time, to a strainer. Rinse quickly with cold water. Now it is ready to cook, soak, or roast.

To make rice more digestible, it may be soaked two to four hours or overnight. To do this, place the rice, plus the recommended amount of cooking water, in a bowl and cover with a bamboo mat to keep out impurities. Do not add salt or other seasoning while soaking. You may use the soaking water to cook in or discard it and use fresh water, especially if the rice is nonorganic. Rice may also be cooked without soaking in a pressure cooker.

BOILED RICE

SERVES 3–4 *(see photo on page 26)*

Boiling is the standard way of preparing rice for daily cooking. Preferably it is cooked in a heavy pot (cast iron, ceramic, or thick-bottomed stainless steel) for the most satisfying results.

1 cup brown rice

pinch of sea salt or 1-inch square piece kombu

1. Sort, wash, and soak rice in 2 cups of water overnight.
2. In a heavy pot, place brown rice and soaking water.
3. Bring to a boil over medium-high flame and add sea salt or kombu. Cover, reduce flame to low, place a flame deflector under the pot, and simmer about 50 minutes or until all the water has been absorbed. Do not open the cover while cooking the rice.
4. Remove from flame and let stand for 10 minutes with lid on.
5. Gently mix cooked rice and transfer to a serving bowl.

VARIATION | You can cook rice with millet, barley, quinoa, or other grains. Usually rice accounts for 70 to 90 percent and the other grain 10 to 30 percent. Sort, wash, and soak grains together and boil or pressure cook as usual.

PRESSURE-COOKED BROWN RICE

SERVES 3–4

Pressure-cooked rice has a satisfying taste and creates a very peaceful feeling. Pressure-cooking is ideal for strong, nourishing rice, especially in cooler and colder weather and seasons, and for healing and medicinal dishes.

1 cup brown rice

pinch of sea salt or 1-inch square piece kombu

1. Sort, wash, and soak rice in 1½ cups of water for several hours or overnight. Reserve soaking water.
2. In a pressure cooker, combine rice, soaking water, and sea salt or kombu. Close pressure cooker lid and bring up to pressure over a medium-high flame.
3. Place a flame deflector underneath the pot, reduce flame to low, and cook for 50 minutes.
4. Remove from flame and let pressure come down naturally.
5. Open lid and mix gently. Transfer to a serving bowl.

VEGETABLE FRIED RICE

SERVES 2-3

Fried rice is a perfect dish for utilizing leftovers and whatever vegetables you have in stock. You can vary the ingredients, adding, for instance, corn kernels in summer and root vegetables in winter.

RICE AND VEGETABLES

1–1½ tablespoons sesame oil

1 teaspoon minced ginger (optional)

1 cup diced onion

several pinches of sea salt

½ cup thinly sliced mushrooms

⅓ cup diced carrots

⅓ cup sliced lotus root (thin quarter moons)

2 cups cooked brown rice

sliced scallions, for garnish

SAVORY SAUCE

2–3 teaspoons shoyu

1 teaspoon brown rice vinegar or lemon juice

1 teaspoon mirin (optional)

1. Heat oil in a skillet and add ginger, onion, and a few pinches of sea salt. Sauté until onion becomes translucent. Add mushrooms and a few more pinches of sea salt, stirring constantly. Add carrots and lotus root, and continue stirring for a few minutes.

2. Place cooked brown rice on top of vegetables. Cover, reduce flame to medium-low, and steam for 2–3 minutes until rice is hot. Add a little water if rice is dry or if the food begins to stick to the skillet.

3. Continue sautéing until the liquid is evaporated and all the ingredients are harmonized well in the skillet.

4. Make the savory sauce by mixing the ingredients in a small bowl. Pour sauce over the rice and veggies. Mix gently for 2–3 minutes. Remove from flame and serve with garnish.

CHEF'S TIP: *Adding minced garlic creates a rich flavor. You can also vary the seasoning by using umeboshi vinegar or apple cider vinegar. Adding a little sauerkraut at the end creates a nice flavor as well. If you use a wok, you can omit the steaming. Instead, sauté the ingredients actively using a higher flame. This style is more energizing.*

BROWN RICE WITH BLACK HOKKAIDO SOYBEANS

SERVES **4–5**

This rice is a rich and satisfying blend of rice and beans. Hokkaido beans are from the northernmost island of Japan and are especially hearty and delicious. This dish nourishes the kidneys, bladder, and reproductive systems and also tones the nervous system.

1½ cups short-grain brown rice

½ cup Hokkaido black soybeans

pinch of sea salt or 1-inch square piece kombu

1. Sort, wash, and soak rice in 1½ cups of water overnight. Reserve soaking water. Using the same amount of water, repeat with soybeans in a separate container.
2. In a pressure cooker, place rice with its soaking water. Drain the soybeans and measure discarded soybean soaking water. Add soybeans, sea salt or kombu, and fresh water equivalent to the amount discarded from the soybean soaking water to the pressure cooker.
3. Close pressure cooker, and bring up to pressure on a medium-high flame.
4. Place a flame deflector underneath the pot, reduce flame to low, and cook for 45–50 minutes.
5. Remove from flame, and let pressure come down naturally. Open lid and mix gently. Transfer to a serving bowl.

"In Sanskrit, there is a word chetana *that means 'innate intelligence in food.' Nowhere is this innate intelligence more apparent than within brown rice and other cereal grains."*
—EDWARD ESKO

SOFT RICE PORRIDGE

SERVES 2–3

Rice porridge is enjoyed as a main breakfast dish around the world. In macrobiotic households, this tasty dish is served several mornings a week. It gives a strong, vitalizing start to the day, stimulates the appetite, and regulates digestion.

1 cup leftover brown rice

1. Combine rice and ½ cup of water in a pot. Cover and bring to a boil.
2. Place a flame deflector underneath the pot, reduce flame to low, and cook for 10–15 minutes. If porridge looks dry, add up to an additional ½ cup of water.
3. Remove cover and spoon porridge into serving bowls.
4. Serve as is or with a condiment.

BROWN RICE WITH CHESTNUTS

The combination of brown rice and chestnuts is a year-round favorite. The natural sweetness of the chestnuts is very soothing and tones the tissues and nervous system.

¾ cup brown rice

¼ cup sweet brown rice

¼ cup dried chestnuts

pinch of sea salt

1. Soak both brown rice and sweet rice together in 1½ cups of water overnight. Soak chestnuts separately in ½ cup of water overnight. Reserve all soaking water.
2. Before cooking, remove brown chestnut skins, if there are any.
3. In a pressure cooker, combine rice mixture, chestnuts, all soaking water, and a pinch of sea salt. Close pressure cooker lid and bring up to pressure over medium-high flame.
4. Place a flame deflector underneath the pot, reduce flame to low, and cook for 45 minutes.
5. Remove from flame, and let pressure come down naturally.
6. Open lid and mix gently. Transfer to a serving bowl.

GOMOKU GOHAN (JAPANESE PILAF)

SERVES 4–5

Gomoku gohan means "five items rice" in Japanese and is a pilaf made with seasonal vegetables cooked with rice. Preparation involves cooking the rice in a savory broth with a variety of ingredients to create a dish with a rich, satisfying umami flavor. The most popular *gomoku gohan* is autumn-style with mushrooms and root vegetables.

PILAF

1 cup brown rice

½ cup sweet brown rice

1 cup SHIITAKE BROTH (page 98)

3 pieces dried shiitake mushrooms, soaked until soft (about 30 minutes), thinly sliced

2 pieces dried tofu, submerged in water until soft (about 10 minutes), water squeezed out, and cut into thin rectangular slices

2 cups chopped root vegetables such as burdock, carrots, or lotus root (matchsticks)

SEASONING

2 tablespoons shoyu (or 1½ tablespoons tamari)

1 tablespoon mirin

¼ teaspoon sea salt

1. Sort, wash, and soak grains together in 1 cup of water overnight. Reserve soaking water.
2. Combine rice, soaking water, and shiitake broth in a pressure cooker.
3. Add the seasoning ingredients to the pressure cooker and stir well.
4. Place shiitake mushrooms, dried tofu slices, and root vegetables on top.
5. Cover with lid and bring up to pressure with a medium flame. Place a flame deflector underneath the pot, reduce flame to low, and cook for 50 minutes.
6. Remove from flame and let pressure come down naturally. Remove lid, mix gently, and serve.

VARIATION | Instead of dried tofu, you can use ½ cup of diced sweet potatoes or corn kernels.

WILD RICE SALAD

SERVES 3-4

Wild rice is a wild grass native to the Great Lakes region that grows in water and has been foraged by native tribes. This recipe uses balsamic vinaigrette to make a California fusion dish with wild rice. The long, thin, dark grains have a slightly nutty flavor and chewy texture, making this salad absolutely delightful.

pinch of sea salt

1 cup wild rice, washed

½ cup thinly sliced celery

½ cup slivered almonds

¼ cup raisins

½ cup finely chopped parsley

DRESSING

1 tablespoon olive oil

1½ tablespoons balsamic vinegar

1 tablespoon lemon juice

2 teaspoons shoyu or tamari

1. In a saucepan, bring 2 cups of water to a boil. Add a pinch of sea salt and wild rice. Cover and bring back to a boil, reduce the flame to low, and simmer for 40 minutes or until the rice become tender. Drain and place the rice in a mixing bowl.
2. Mix the dressing ingredients.
3. Add dressing to the wild rice and gently mix well. Add celery, almonds, raisins, and parsley.
4. Taste and adjust the seasoning and serve.

VEGETABLE PAELLA

This vegan paella is simple to prepare, yet enticing in aroma and flavor.

3 tablespoons olive oil

1 large onion, diced

1 clove garlic

2 cups sliced white mushrooms

1 cup diced bell peppers (red for color)

1 cup chopped string beans (1-inch lengths)

1 teaspoon sea salt, divided

2½ cups VEGETABLE BROTH (page 98) or water

½ teaspoon saffron, soaked with 2 tablespoons water

1 teaspoon turmeric powder

1½ cups basmati brown rice, sorted, washed, and soaked for 30 minutes then drained

kalamata olives, thinly sliced, for topping

parsley, for garnish

1. Heat olive oil in a large skillet or frying pan, and sauté onion until translucent and tender. Add garlic, mushrooms, bell peppers, and string beans, and continue sautéing for a few more minutes. Add ½ teaspoon of sea salt.

2. Add vegetable broth or water, the rest of the sea salt, the saffron with its soaking water, and turmeric powder. Bring to a boil over a medium flame. Carefully add basmati rice and return to a boil.

3. Reduce flame to low, place flame deflector underneath skillet, cover, and simmer for 45–60 minutes until the rice becomes tender and most of the liquid is absorbed.

4. Turn off flame, remove from stovetop, and leave the cover on for 10 minutes to steam the paella. Top with kalamata olives and serve with parsley for garnish.

CHEF'S TIP: *If you would like to add more protein to the paella, add tempeh, seitan, or cooked beans such as chickpeas.*

MUSHROOM AND LEEK RISOTTO

SERVES 4–5

This risotto is adapted from a recipe by Patricio Garcia de Paredes, a renowned macrobiotic chef. While traditional risotto requires a labor-intensive process of adding water incrementally, this dish employs a simpler approach to achieve the creamy risotto consistency.

RISOTTO

1–2 tablespoons extra-virgin olive oil

1 garlic clove, minced

1 small onion, finely diced

½ small leek, rinsed well and thinly sliced

1½ cups thinly sliced brown or white mushrooms

½ teaspoon sea salt, plus more to taste

¼ cup sake (optional)

3 cups VEGETABLE BROTH (page 98) or water

3 cups cooked brown rice

1 tablespoon white miso

black pepper (optional)

GARNISH

fresh lettuce leaves

BALSAMIC REDUCTION SAUCE (page 225) (optional)

1. Heat oil and sauté the garlic for 1 minute. Add the onion and sauté until soft.

2. Add the leek, mushrooms, and sea salt and continue to sauté for about 5 minutes.

3. Add sake, if using, and vegetable broth or water, and bring to a boil. Reduce flame to medium-low, add salt to taste, and cook for 10–15 minutes or until a nicely seasoned flavor develops.

4. Add the cooked brown rice and continue to cook over a medium-low flame while constantly stirring with a wooden spoon. Add more water if too thick, and keep stirring until creamy consistency.

5. Reduce flame to low, and add miso and black pepper, if using. Keep simmering for 5 minutes. Adjust to taste if needed.

6. Serve topped with lettuce leaves and balsamic reduction sauce, if desired.

CHEF'S TIP: *You may also use dried shiitake or porcini mushroom in the risotto. Use the mushroom soaking water for broth.*

VEGETABLE SUSHI ROLLS

MAKES 3 ROLLS

Sushi rolls are great for parties and for food to go. You may use different seasonal vegetables inside sushi rolls. Or to make tempeh sushi rolls, add SAVORY TEMPEH STRIPS (page 152) along with vegetables.

BROWN RICE SUSHI

1 cup short-grain brown rice, washed and soaked overnight with 1½ cups water

1-inch square piece kombu

SUSHI ROLLS

3 sheets sushi nori

umeboshi paste, to taste

1 medium carrot and 3 scallions, sliced lengthwise and blanched

1 medium cucumber, seeded and sliced lengthwise into thin strips

3 tablespoons sauerkraut

WASABI DIPPING SAUCE (page 85) (optional)

TO MAKE BROWN SUSHI RICE:

1. Combine rice, soaking water, and kombu in a pressure cooker, and bring to a boil. Close the pressure cooker lid and bring up to pressure. Place flame deflector under the pressure cooker, and simmer for 50 minutes.

2. Remove from flame, and let pressure come down naturally. Open lid, and transfer the rice into a moistened wood sushi bowl or onto a big glass plate. With a wet rice paddle, gently mix, and let cool to slightly warmer than room temperature. Keep the rice covered with a damp towel until ready to use.

TO MAKE SUSHI ROLLS:

1. On a sushi mat, place a sheet of nori smooth side down. Wet your hands and spread a thin layer of rice evenly on the nori sheet, leaving 1 inch at the bottom and 3 inches at the top of the nori sheet uncovered.

2. Spread a small amount of umeboshi paste horizontally across the middle of rice. Place some slices of carrot, scallion, and cucumber on top of the paste. Place 1 tablespoon of sauerkraut on top of the vegetables.

3. Placing your thumbs behind the sushi mat, and while holding the rice on the nori, begin rolling forward. Make sure the filling is in its place, tucked in while rolling. Roll into a sushi roll and use a sharp knife to cut it into rounds, about 1-inch thick each.

4. Repeat steps 1–3 two more times to make three sushi rolls total.

5. Serve as is or with wasabi dipping sauce.

OHAGI

Ohagi are small rice balls prepared with sweet rice and different fillings and toppings. In Japan they are traditionally made in autumn to celebrate the harvest and express gratitude to past generations. As a little girl, Sachi was taught how to make ohagi by her grandmother. Here are the two most popular kinds of ohagi. One is wrapped with sweet azuki paste and the other with kinako (roasted soybean powder).

OHAGI RICE

1 cup sweet brown rice

pinch of sea salt

SWEET AZUKI BEANS

1 cup azuki beans

¼ cup dried apricot

1-inch square piece kombu

⅛–¼ teaspoon sea salt

¼ cup brown rice syrup, or to taste

KINAKO / SOYBEAN POWDER MIXTURE

¼ cup kinako (roasted soybean powder)

1 tablespoon maple sugar (optional)

⅛ teaspoon sea salt

VARIATIONS | Feel free to create your own ohagi variations, such as covering with seeds and nuts, or topping or filling with sweet potato paste

TO MAKE OHAGI RICE:

1. Sort, wash, and soak rice in 1½ cups of water overnight.
2. Place rice, soaking water, and sea salt in a pressure cooker, close the lid, and bring up to pressure.
3. Place a flame deflector underneath the pot and cook for 50 minutes. Remove from flame and let pressure come down completely.
4. Open the lid and pound the rice for 10–15 minutes with a pestle.
5. Let the rice cool down. Then make small rice balls.

TO MAKE SWEET AZUKI BEANS:

1. Wash and soak azuki beans in 2 cups water overnight. Place azuki, its soaking water, dried apricot, and kombu in a heavy pot and bring to a boil.
2. Cook the beans for about 45 minutes to 1 hour until soft. Add ¼ cup of cold water to shock the beans as cooking water becomes low.
3. Add sea salt and brown rice syrup, stirring gently. If you need more of a sweet taste, you can add a little more brown rice syrup.
4. Cook until bean mixture turns firm and pasty but not runny. Set aside to cool to room temperature.

TO MAKE OHAGI BALLS:

1. To make bean ohagi, make small rice balls, and then wrap the outside of the rice with the bean mixture. Wetting your hands prevents them from sticking to the rice.
2. To make kinako ohagi, first mix the ingredients for the kinako in a small bowl. Form the bean mixture into a ball, then wrap with rice, and finally roll the ball in kinako mixture, covering completely.

PAN-FRIED MOCHI

SERVES **4**

Mochi, or sweet rice that is pounded into cakes or small squares, gives sustainable energy and makes a great snack. It is available in select natural foods stores or can be made at home. Mochi can be served savory or sweet. Here is a savory version.

2–3 teaspoons sesame oil

4 mochi pieces, each piece 3 inches by 2 inches

shoyu or tamari

grated daikon (optional)

nori sheet, cut into smaller strips for wrapping each piece of mochi

1. Heat a cast-iron or heavy stainless-steel skillet. Place sesame oil and then mochi in the skillet.
2. Reduce flame to medium-low, and slowly brown one side of the mochi. Turn the mochi pieces over, cover skillet, and brown the other side. As the mochi browns, it will puff up.
3. When it puffs up and both sides are browned, remove and place on a serving plate. Sprinkle a few drops of shoyu or tamari on top, garnish with a little grated daikon over the mochi, and wrap with nori strips. Serve while warm.

CHEF'S TIP: *For a sweet snack, drizzle with brown rice or maple syrup, or eat with apple butter. Mochi also goes well in soups. Place two or three pieces of cooked mochi in soups toward the end of cooking. You can also deep-fry mochi, which is delicious. Fry until crispy and the color turns golden. Serve with a little shoyu and grated daikon to help digest the oil.*

MOCHI WAFFLES WITH LEMON SYRUP

SERVES 2-3

Mochi waffles are delicious, energize us in our midafternoons, and are so easy to make!

MOCHI

8 ounces mochi

LEMON SYRUP

3 tablespoons brown rice
  syrup

2 tablespoons water

pinch of sea salt

1 teaspoon lemon juice

1 tablespoon lemon zest

1. Preheat a waffle iron or waffle maker.

2. Grate or thinly slice mochi.

3. Place a handful of sliced mochi into each waffle mold. Cook until the mochi puffs up and turns slightly crispy. Repeat this process with each waffle.

4. While the waffles are cooking, place brown rice syrup, water, and a pinch of sea salt in a small saucepan. Bring to a boil, reduce flame to low, and simmer for a few minutes.

5. Remove from the stovetop, add lemon juice and lemon zest, and mix gently.

6. As soon as the mochi waffles are done, serve immediately with lemon syrup.

Millet with Winter Squash
(see recipe on page 63)

WHOLE GRAINS: BARLEY, MILLET, QUINOA, AND OTHERS

"As the farmer casts into the ground the finest ears of his grain, the time will come when we too shall hold nothing back, but shall eagerly convert more than we now possess into means and powers, when we shall be willing to sow the sun and the moon for seeds."
—RALPH WALDO EMERSON, *MAN THE REFORMER*

BESIDES BROWN RICE, THERE ARE MANY OTHER WHOLE GRAINS THAT ARE A HEALTHY, energizing part of a balanced diet. We serve millet and barley regularly, by themselves or combined with other grains, beans, or vegetables, and as ingredients in soups, stews, baked goods, snacks, or desserts. Several times a week, we also serve oats, whole wheat berries, maize, quinoa, amaranth, *hato mugi*, buckwheat, and other grains and cereals.

BARLEY

Native to the Mediterranean, barley was the staple of ancient Greece, Egypt, Israel, and Mesopotamia, as well as the British Isles and parts of Central Europe. In addition to grain, porridge, soups, and stews, it was baked into bread and brewed into beer. In North America, barley arrived with the Pilgrims on the *Mayflower* and supplemented maize as the principal grain in New England.

Whole-grain barley is the hardiest and most energizing type. It takes longer to cook and is chewier than pearled barley. It was the principal food recommended by Hippocrates to prevent and relieve common ailments. Pearled barley, or ordinary barley, is lightly refined. Its aleurone, or outer layer of endosperm, has been removed. It is still suitable for occasional use, but for strong, vitalizing energy whole-grain barley is preferred.

MILLET

Millet is eaten regularly by one-third of the people on the planet and is the fourth most abundant crop after wheat, rice, and maize. As scientific studies show, among its many physical and mental benefits, millet helps to prevent heart disease, cancer, and many other chronic diseases. It helps stabilize the emotions and, according to several recent macrobiotic medical studies, lowers blood sugar levels and is effective in treating diabetes.

Millet comes in various shapes, sizes, and colors, ranging from pale yellow to golden (in the Far East), red (India), white and black (Africa), and even green (America). Relative to rice and other grains, millet seeds are tiny. But the variations among millets are substantial, yielding seeds that can be small, medium, or large. Foxtail millet, the most common type of millet, is yellow and widely available in natural foods stores and select supermarkets. It is the type we use regularly.

OATS

Oats make a warm, nourishing breakfast porridge and are a principal grain in Scotland, Ireland, and other parts of the British Isles. Whole oats or oats groats give the strongest, most vitalizing energy, especially in winter or cold weather. Steel-cut oats have been cut into smaller pieces and give moderate energy, while rolled oats or oat flakes give light upward energy.

WHEAT

Wheat, the most consumed grain on the planet, originated in the Fertile Crescent and spread around the world. Today it is also the main grain in China, especially the central and northern regions, where it displaced millet. Common varieties of wheat include hard red winter wheat that makes for stronger, firmer flour and is used mostly for bread and baked goods. Soft durum wheat is ideal for noodles, dumplings, and pasta. In addition to these popular foods, whole-grain wheat, known as wheat berries, may be eaten by themselves or combined with other grains.

MAIZE

Maize, or Indian corn, originated in ancient Mexico and Guatemala. It initially spread to North and South America and eventually worldwide.

We use corn year-round. In summer and autumn, we enjoy corn on the cob. In cooler seasons, we enjoy tortillas, arepas (corn masa cakes), polenta, corn bread, and other dishes. It is important to obtain heirloom varieties as much as possible because most corn, including organic, is hybrid, and about 90 percent of corn grown in the United States is GMO.

QUINOA

Quinoa, the Mother Grain of the Incas, is traditionally grown in terraced fields in Peru, Bolivia, Ecuador, and Colombia. Its tiny seeds are high in protein and are a rich source of B vitamins, vitamin E, minerals, and trace elements. Quinoa cooks up soft and fluffy. White, ivory, or golden quinoa is the most common type. Red quinoa holds its shape better in cooking than white and is used in salads and other distinct dishes. Black quinoa is earthier and sweeter than the other types and gives a slightly firmer texture. Quinoa products include flour, flakes, and pasta. Quinoa is gluten-free and a preferred grain for those who are gluten sensitive.

WHOLE BARLEY SOUP

SERVES 3–4

This creamy barley soup is smooth, soothing, and a great springtime dish for cleansing our bodies. Barley strengthens the liver and boosts the body's detoxing power.

WHOLE BARLEY

1 cup whole barley, sorted, washed, and soaked with 2 cups water overnight, reserve soaking water

pinch of sea salt

SOUP

1 tablespoon sesame oil

1 medium onion, diced (1½ cups)

few pinches of sea salt

1 cup diced mushrooms

¼ cup diced carrots

2½ cups VEGETABLE BROTH (page 98) or water

1 teaspoon grated ginger

1 tablespoon white miso

scallions or parsley, for garnish

TO COOK WHOLE BARLEY:

1. Place whole barley with soaking water and sea salt in a pressure cooker.
2. Close the pressure cooker lid, bring up pressure, place flame deflector underneath the pot, reduce flame to low, and simmer for 1 hour.
3. Remove from flame and let the pressure come down naturally.
4. Open the lid and gently mix.

TO MAKE THE SOUP:

1. Heat oil in a heavy pot, add onion with a few pinches of sea salt, and sauté until translucent. Add mushrooms and carrots, and sauté until mushrooms become soft.
2. Add vegetable broth or water and 1 cup of cooked barley. Bring to a boil, cover the pot, reduce flame to low, and simmer for 40–50 minutes until the soup becomes creamy.
3. Add ginger, then dissolve miso in a small bowl by adding a small amount of broth. Season with white miso, and simmer for a few minutes on low flame.
4. Serve with garnish.

PEARLED BARLEY OJIYA

SERVES 2–3

Ojiya, a Japanese-style seasoned porridge with vegetables, is a popular breakfast dish.

PEARLED BARLEY

1 cup pearled barely,
    soaked with 2 cups
    water overnight, reserve
    soaking water

pinch of sea salt

OJIYA

1 cup cooked pearled barley

¼ cup diced onion

2 tablespoons diced carrots

2 tablespoons diced celery

1 tablespoon sliced leek

½–1 tablespoon barley miso

scallions, for garnish

TO MAKE THE PEARLED BARLEY:

1. Place pearled barley with soaking water and sea salt in a saucepan.
2. Bring to a boil, cover, reduce flame to low, and simmer for 45–50 minutes.
3. Remove from flame and let steam or stand for 10 minutes.
4. Gently mix the cooked grains.

TO MAKE THE OJIYA:

1. Place cooked pearled barley and ⅔ cup of water in a medium saucepan and bring to a boil.
2. Add onion, carrots, celery, and leek. Cover and simmer for 10 minutes or until vegetables become soft. If you desire a soupier consistency, add a little more water, and continue to simmer until it becomes hot.
3. Reduce flame to low and dissolve miso in a small bowl by adding a small amount of broth. Add miso to the pot. Adjust the flavor if necessary. Keep simmering for 5 more minutes.
4. Serve with garnish.

TANGY BARLEY SALAD WITH LEMON-SHALLOT VINAIGRETTE

SERVES **4**

This is a super dish for springtime. The liver is the most active organ during this season. Barley and a sour, tangy flavor help open up the overburdened or stagnated liver and strengthen its natural detoxing power.

2–3 red radishes, thinly sliced

dash of umeboshi vinegar

2 cups cooked whole barley

4 kalamata olives, thinly sliced

⅓ cup minced parsley

⅓ cup LEMON-SHALLOT VINAIGRETTE (page 193)

1. In a bowl, massage radishes with a dash of umeboshi vinegar, and set aside until water comes out. Squeeze out excess liquid and discard.

2. In another mixing bowl, combine cooked whole barley, radishes, olives, parsley, and vinaigrette. Mix gently to harmonize all the ingredients together.

3. Serve immediately or let marinate for another day and use later. Marinating overnight will enhance its flavor.

COUSCOUS SALAD

SERVES 3-4

This is a dynamic and summery grain salad. You will be absolutely delighted with its light, cooling energy and rich, nutty taste.

COUSCOUS SALAD

pinch of sea salt

1 tablespoon olive oil

1 cup whole wheat couscous

1½ tablespoons dried currants

¼ cup finely diced red onion, massaged with a few drops of umeboshi vinegar

½ cup finely diced cucumber, massaged with a few pinches of sea salt

1 cup diced sweet potatoes, roasted in 350°F oven until soft (optional)

½ cup minced parsley

1 tablespoon lemon zest

2 tablespoons coarsely chopped roasted pecans

CITRUS MAPLE DRESSING

2 tablespoons maple syrup

3 tablespoons olive oil

5-6 tablespoons lemon juice

4 teaspoons umeboshi vinegar

dash of black pepper (optional)

1. Combine 1¼ cups of water, sea salt, and olive oil in a medium saucepan and bring to a boil.
2. Add couscous, mix with a whisk, and cover.
3. Turn off flame and let stand for 10 minutes.
4. In the meantime, make the citrus dressing by mixing all the ingredients.
5. Fluff the couscous, transfer it into a large mixing bowl, and let cool.
6. Add currants and the citrus dressing to taste to the couscous, and mix gently. Adjust the amount of dressing if necessary.
7. Drain excess water from the red onion and cucumber, and add to the couscous (along with roasted sweet potatoes, if using).
8. Add parsley, lemon zest, and pecans, gently mixing everything.

VARIATIONS | For variations, add roasted beets, olives, blanched kale, or raisins. A touch of orange juice is also nice added to the dressing.

HATO MUGI SALAD WITH MISO-TAHINI DRESSING

SERVES 4–5

This delicious salad could be called Beauty Grain Salad! Hato mugi (also known as pearl barley and Job's Tears) has the unique property of discharging toxins from the body. It also makes the skin shiny and silky. In Japan, in addition to eating it, women traditionally make face masks with cooked hato mugi.

HATO MUGI SALAD

1 cup hato mugi, rinsed and soaked with 2 cups water overnight, reserve soaking water

pinch of sea salt

½ cup minced red onion

½ cup sliced carrots (thin matchsticks)

½ cup sliced red radish (thin half-moons)

1 teaspoon umeboshi vinegar

1 cup fresh or frozen corn kernels

6–8 pickled olives, pitted and sliced thin

⅓ cup finely chopped parsley

MISO-TAHINI DRESSING

¼ cup white miso

3 tablespoons tahini

¼ cup lemon juice

¼ cup water

1–2 teaspoons shoyu

1. In a heavy pot, place hato mugi and its soaking water. Bring to a boil and add sea salt. Cover, reduce flame to low, place a flame deflector under the pot, and simmer until soft, about 45 minutes to 1 hour. Place cooked hato mugi in a large bowl, and let cool to room temperature.

2. In individual bowls, place onion, carrots, and radish with umeboshi vinegar and marinate for 15–30 minutes. This enables the vegetable cells to break down and aids in digestion. Also, the colors become vibrant.

3. In a separate small saucepan, bring 2 cups of water to a boil and blanch corn kernels. Strain corn kernels in a bowl and let cool.

4. Make miso-tahini dressing by mixing all the dressing ingredients in a suribachi or bowl. Adjust the flavor and consistency according to your preference.

5. Place all the vegetables, corn kernels, marinade juice, pickled olives, and parsley into the hato mugi bowl. Gently mix to harmonize all the ingredients together.

6. Serve with miso-tahini dressing.

CHEF'S TIP: *Hato mugi naturally has a slightly bitter taste. By combining with sweet-flavored vegetables such as corn, carrots, and onions, as well as a creamy dressing, the bitter flavor turns milder and harmonizes well with other flavors in the salad.*

millet with sweet vegetable soup

MILLET WITH SWEET VEGETABLE SOUP

SERVES **4–5**

This sweet, creamy soup is a favorite year-round. The chickpea miso also enhances the sweet flavor.

½ cup millet, soaked with 3 cups water overnight, reserve soaking water

1 cup finely diced sweet vegetables (squash, onions, carrots, cauliflower, cabbage, etc.)

pinch of sea salt

1–1½ tablespoons chickpea miso

scallions, for garnish

1. In a heavy pot, combine millet and diced vegetables with soaking water. Bring to a boil and add sea salt.
2. Cover, place a flame deflector underneath pot, reduce flame to low, and simmer for 30–40 minutes until millet becomes soft and creamy.
3. Season with miso. Continue to simmer for 5 minutes.
4. Serve with garnish.

MILLET WITH WINTER SQUASH

SERVES **5–6** *(see photo on page 50)*

This delicious preparation is one of the most nourishing dishes for the pancreas and spleen. It provides a naturally sweet taste and helps stabilize blood sugar levels. We suggest that you incorporate it in your weekly menu, especially in late summer and autumn. This dish also makes a great breakfast porridge. Add sufficient water to create your desired consistency.

1 cup millet, washed and soaked with 4 cups water overnight, reserve soaking water

2 cups chopped winter squash (such as kabocha or butternut squash) (bite-size pieces)

pinch of sea salt

shiso powder (optional)

parsley, for garnish (optional)

1. In a saucepan, combine millet with its soaking water and winter squash. Bring to a boil, and add sea salt.
2. Cover, place a flame deflector underneath the pot, and simmer for 30 minutes until the millet and squash become soft and creamy.
3. Serve plain or with shiso condiment or garnish with parsley.

MILLET CROQUETTES

SERVES 3–4 (MAKES 6–8 CROQUETTES)

Everybody loves these crispy pan-fried patties. And when you have leftover millet stew or millet mashed potatoes, you can make these croquettes the next day.

2 cups thinly sliced cauliflower

⅔ cup millet, soaked with 3 cups water overnight, reserve soaking water

pinch of sea salt

2 tablespoons grated carrots

1 tablespoon toasted black sesame seeds

1 cup seasonal vegetables (corn, peas, squash, etc.)

½ cup chopped parsley

safflower oil, for pan-frying

TOFU SOUR CREAM (page 227) or TOFU TARTAR SAUCE (page 226), for topping

1. Layer cauliflower on the bottom of a heavy pot, followed by millet.
2. Gently add the millet soaking water. Bring to a boil, add sea salt, and cover. Reduce flame to low and place a flame deflector underneath the pot. Cook for about 40 minutes until millet becomes soft.
3. While millet is cooking, blanch seasonal vegetables.
4. When millet is done, mash and let cool for about 15 minutes until the temperature is warm but cool enough to handle. If you let the mixture cool to room temperature, millet will set so that it is not suitable to form patties.
5. Combine millet with blanched vegetables and other ingredients and form rounded croquettes. Pan-fry with sesame oil on both sides until a nice golden color.
6. Serve with tofu sour cream or tofu tartar sauce.

"If you can look into the seeds of time, and say which grain will grow and which will not, speak then unto me."

—MARLOWE AND SHAKESPEARE, *MACBETH*

MILLET MASHED POTATOES WITH SHIITAKE GRAVY

SERVES 5-6

Millet with cauliflower, a classic macrobiotic dish, cooks up soft and creamy and even tastes like mashed potatoes. The shiitake gravy makes it especially tasty.

2 cups thinly sliced cauliflower

1 cup millet, washed and soaked with 4 cups water overnight, reserve soaking water

pinch of sea salt

1 tablespoon tahini (optional)

¼ cup soy milk or other nondairy milk (optional)

SHIITAKE GRAVY (below)

parsley, for garnish

1. In a saucepan, layer in the cauliflower first, then add the millet with its soaking water. Bring to a boil over a medium flame and add a pinch of sea salt. Cover, place a flame deflector underneath the pot, and simmer for 30–40 minutes until millet becomes soft and creamy.

2. Remove from flame and mash the millet and cauliflower with a potato masher until the texture becomes smooth.

3. In a small bowl, mix tahini with soy milk. Add to the cauliflower-millet mixture. Continue to mix well until the texture becomes like mashed potatoes.

4. Serve with shiitake gravy and parsley for garnish.

SHIITAKE GRAVY

MAKES 1 CUP

3–4 dried shiitake mushrooms, soaked with 2 cups water for ½–1 hour

1–2 teaspoons sesame oil

½ medium onion, diced

pinch of sea salt

1 teaspoon minced ginger

1 tablespoon shoyu, or to taste

1½ tablespoons kuzu, dissolved in 2 tablespoons cold water

minced parsley, for garnish

1. Slice soaked shiitake mushrooms thinly and set aside. Reserve soaking water.

2. In a saucepan, heat sesame oil and sauté onion with sea salt for 3–4 minutes, until translucent.

3. Add shiitake soaking water, ginger, and shiitake mushrooms, and bring back to a boil. Cover, reduce flame to low, and simmer for 10 minutes.

4. Season with shoyu and add dissolved kuzu mixture. Stir until broth thickens and becomes translucent. Simmer for another 10 minutes.

5. Garnish with parsley and serve.

FLUFFY QUINOA SALAD

SERVES 5-6

This tasty salad has a rich, satisfying flavor as is, but can also be enhanced with zesty CILANTRO SAUCE (page 227).

QUINOA SALAD

1 cup quinoa, sorted and washed

pinch of sea salt

½ tablespoon lemon zest

1 tablespoon lemon juice

½ cup chopped parsley or fresh mint, for garnish

DRESSING

1 tablespoon olive oil

¼ teaspoon sea salt

1 teaspoon ginger juice

TO MAKE THE QUINOA:

1. Combine quinoa and 1¾ cups of water in a medium pot. Bring to a boil, and add sea salt. Place flame deflector underneath, then simmer for 20 minutes. Remove from flame and let stand for 10 minutes.

2. Transfer to a bowl and let cool.

TO MAKE THE DRESSING:

1. Place olive oil, sea salt, and ¼ cup of water in a saucepan.

2. Bring to a boil and simmer for a minute, and then add ginger juice.

3. Remove from flame and let cool for a few minutes.

TO COMBINE:

1. Toss the dressing over the quinoa and mix gently.

2. Add lemon zest, lemon juice, and parsley for garnish.

3. Serve warm or at room temperature.

teff

TEFF

SERVES 4–5

Teff, a tiny grain from East Africa, looks like chocolate when cooked. This basic recipe makes a rich, creamy porridge with a soft consistency.

1 cup teff

pinch of sea salt

toasted walnuts or sunflower seeds, for topping

1. Combine teff and 4 cups of water in a medium-size pot and bring to a boil. Add sea salt.
2. Place a flame deflector underneath, reduce flame to medium-low, cover, and simmer for 30–40 minutes until thick and creamy. In order to prevent clumping, stir frequently during the first 10 minutes of cooking and periodically throughout the remainder of the cooking process.
3. Serve with toasted sunflower seeds or walnuts.

VARIATION | Toasting teff in a skillet for 5 minutes before cooking with water is also nice for a rich flavor. Add 2 tablespoons of sorghum syrup (a traditional African sweetener), brown rice syrup, or barley malt to sweeten.

AMARANTH PORRIDGE

SERVES 4

Amaranth, native to South and Central America, has beautiful wavy stalks and bright purple blossoms. This morning porridge packs a protein punch, and its creamy-crunchy texture is unique. Mineral-rich, gluten-free amaranth is nourishing and tasty.

1 cup amaranth

pinch of sea salt

roasted pumpkin seeds and/or sunflower seeds (optional)

1. Place amaranth in a fine strainer and place a medium bowl underneath. Wash with water and drain well. (Avoid a coarse strainer or otherwise the tiny amaranth grains will pass through.)
2. Combine amaranth and 4 cups of water in a pot and bring to a boil. Add sea salt.
3. Place a flame deflector underneath the pot. Reduce flame to low, cover, and simmer for 25–35 minutes, allowing the grain to become tender. Stir amaranth occasionally.
4. Serve in individual serving bowls, and garnish with toasted seeds.

AREPAS (PAN-FRIED CORN MASA CAKES)

MAKES 3 PATTIES

These pan-fried cakes, inspired by a traditional South American maize dish, are easy to make, richly textured, and satisfying. They are a great food or snack for kids and for adults who crave baked food.

1 cup corn masa harina (instant masa, precooked white corn meal)

pinch of sea salt

2 tablespoons safflower oil, plus more for pan-frying

avocado slices, for topping (optional)

1. Place masa, sea salt, oil, and ⅔ cup of water in a mixing bowl. Mix well using hands until mixture forms a soft, moist dough (use more water as necessary). Let the dough sit for 10 minutes, covered with plastic wrap over the bowl.

2. Divide the dough into three parts, and make small oval or round ½ inch flat patties.

3. Heat a cast-iron skillet, add safflower oil, and place patties in the pan. Cover, reduce flame to low, and pan-fry the patties on one side for about 10 minutes until lightly brown.

4. Flip the patties over, cover, and pan-fry the other side for about 10 minutes until the surface becomes crispy and lightly brown.

5. Serve as a side dish or as a snack with a dip. You can also serve with slices of avocado, if desired.

VARIATIONS | In Latin America, arepas are often filled or topped with salad or other ingredients. Try stuffing them with black beans or sea vegetable stew.

Yakisoba (Pan-Fried Soba Noodles)
(see recipe on page 77)

TASTY NOODLES, SPRING ROLLS, DUMPLINGS, AND BREADSTUFFS

"At midnight the temple bell in our village pealed 108 times to welcome in the new year. At this late hour, traditional families throughout Japan celebrated the happy occasion with delicious homemade soba."

—AVELINE KUSHI

FRIED RICE-VERMICELLI

SERVES **3–4** (see photo on page iv)

This dish is inspired by Indonesian stir-fried noodles called *bihun goreng*. Rice-vermicelli noodles can be found in an Asian grocery store. Different from Italian vermicelli, these thin noodles are made from rice. Quick and easy, this dish will fit into your active and busy day. Other types of thin noodles, such as mung bean noodles, can be used instead.

4 ounces Asian rice-vermicelli noodles

1–1½ tablespoons sesame oil

1–2 teaspoons minced ginger

1 cup sliced onion (thin half-moons)

sea salt, to taste

¼ cup finely chopped wood ear mushrooms

½ cup thinly sliced fresh shiitake mushrooms

½ cup sliced carrots (thin matchsticks)

1 cup chopped cabbage (bite-size)

1 tablespoon shoyu

1 teaspoon rice vinegar

sprouts (such as broccoli or alfalfa) or scallions, for garnish

roasted black sesame seeds, for topping

1. In a saucepan, bring 3 cups of water to a boil. Add vermicelli noodles, remove from flame, and let the noodles cook for 5–10 minutes according to the directions on the package. Drain in a strainer.

2. In a skillet, heat sesame oil and sauté ginger and onion with a few pinches of sea salt until onion turns translucent.

3. Add mushrooms and a few pinches of sea salt, and keep sautéing for 3 minutes. Add carrots and cabbage, and continue sautéing for a few more minutes until the vegetables become tender. If the bottom of the skillet becomes dry, add a little water or oil.

4. Add vermicelli noodles, and mix everything gently. Reduce flame to low, add shoyu and rice vinegar, and gently mix again. Continue to simmer for a few minutes.

5. Serve with garnish and black sesame seeds.

CHEF'S TIP: *Wood ear mushrooms are a type of floppy cup-shaped mushroom found in Asia, Africa, South America, and other places around the world. If you use dried wood ear mushrooms, soak for 10 minutes and drain, then boil for 5 minutes before cooking. If unavailable, replace with other mushrooms.*

YAKISOBA (PAN-FRIED SOBA NOODLES)

SERVES **4–5** (see photo on page 74)

These scrumptious pan-fried noodles, known in Japan as *yakisoba*, are widely popular. Tasty, satisfying, and energizing, they make a meal in themselves with vegetables and the rich seasoning sauce.

YAKISOBA

6 ounces soba noodles (makes about 3 cups cooked noodles)

1 tablespoon sesame oil

1 cup sliced onion (thin half-moons)

several pinches of sea salt

½ cup thinly sliced fresh mushrooms (shiitake, button, shimeji, etc.)

½ cup sliced carrots (thin matchsticks)

1 cup thinly sliced celery, on the diagonal

1 cup chopped green vegetables (such as cabbage or radish greens)

1 cup mung bean sprouts

scallions, for garnish

nori strips, for topping

YAKISOBA SAUCE

2 tablespoons shoyu

1 tablespoon lemon juice

1 tablespoon SHIITAKE BROTH (page 98) or water

1 teaspoon toasted sesame oil

1–2 teaspoons ginger juice

1–2 teaspoons mirin

1. In a big pot, cook soba noodles according to the directions on the package. Drain and wash noodles well with cold water. Set aside.

2. In a large skillet, heat sesame oil and sauté onion with a few pinches of sea salt for 4–5 minutes until translucent.

3. Add mushrooms and a few more pinches of sea salt, and continue sautéing for 3–4 minutes. Add carrots and celery, and keep sautéing for 3–4 more minutes. Add green vegetables and continue sautéing, mixing all the vegetables well in the skillet.

4. Add soba noodles on top of the vegetables, cover, and steam for a few minutes on medium-low flame. If the bottom of the skillet is dry, add a little water before covering the skillet.

5. Make yakisoba sauce by combining the ingredients in a small bowl.

6. Open the cover, pour in yakisoba sauce, and toss bean sprouts over the vegetables. Over low flame, mix noodles and vegetables together using tongs. Mix gently so that the noodles don't break but the sauce will penetrate all the ingredients. Adjust the flavor if necessary.

7. Serve with scallions as garnish and nori strips for topping.

VARIATIONS | You may also use udon or other types of noodles. If you are gluten sensitive, use brown rice or quinoa noodles.

CHEF'S TIP: *Use seasonal vegetables as much as possible. For instance, in the summer, you can use fresh corn and summer squash, and for winter, use burdock and other root vegetables.*

NOODLES IN CLEAR BROTH

SERVES 3-4

This recipe is adapted from Aveline Kushi's recipe. The noodle soup is easy and quick to make for a simple one-bowl meal. It has everything—nourishing broth, grain, protein, and vegetables. This noodle soup warms you up and replenishes your energy.

6 ounces noodles (such as soba, udon, or brown rice noodles)

BROTH

2–3-inch piece kombu

2–3 dried shiitake mushrooms

1½–2 tablespoons shoyu, or to taste

one-third a (14-ounce) package tofu, cut into cubes

scallions or toasted nori strips, for garnish

TO MAKE THE NOODLES:

1. Bring 8 cups of water to a boil. Add noodles and return to a boil. Cook the noodles following the instructions on the package, usually 7–10 minutes.

2. Remove the noodles from the pot, drain, and rinse thoroughly with cold water to stop them from cooking and to prevent clumping.

TO MAKE THE BROTH:

1. Put kombu and shiitake mushrooms in a pot and add 4 cups of water.

2. Take out shiitake mushrooms after 15 minutes when they become soft. Then remove the hard part of the stem and slice thinly.

3. Add sliced shiitake back to the pot and bring to a boil. Lower the flame and simmer for 5 minutes.

4. Remove kombu and save for use in other dishes.

5. Add shoyu to taste and simmer for 5 minutes.

6. Put the cooked noodles in the broth to warm them, but do not let them boil. Add tofu cubes and simmer until tofu is thoroughly cooked. When everything gets hot, place noodles in serving bowls, pour the broth, and serve immediately with garnish.

CHEF'S TIP: *A little grated ginger may be added to the broth. Vegetables such as daikon, carrots, and onions, as well as a small volume of sea vegetables such as wakame, also make good additions.*

SOBA NOODLE SALAD WITH TEMPEH AND SESAME DRESSING

Noodle salad is very popular in Japan, especially during the hot summer. Noodles and finely sliced vegetables go well with this tangy, savory sesame dressing, which buoys us up for an active summer day!

SOBA SALAD

8 ounces SAVORY TEMPEH STRIPS (page 152)

2 red bell peppers (optional)

1 cup sliced carrots (matchsticks)

umeboshi vinegar

1 cup sliced cucumber (matchsticks)

3–4 cups vegetables (such as brussels sprouts, corn kernels, kale, and asparagus)

8 ounces soba noodles

fresh lettuce, washed and dried in a salad spinner

scallions, for garnish

SESAME DRESSING

¼ cup shoyu

¼ cup brown rice vinegar

2 tablespoons water

2 teaspoons toasted sesame oil

3 tablespoons coarsely ground toasted tan sesame seeds

1. Make SAVORY TEMPEH STRIPS according to the recipe. Let cool and slice into thin strips.
2. If using, roast whole bell pepper on top of stove over open flame until skin blackens. Let cool, peel skin, and clean under running water. Slice bell pepper into thin strips, and discard the seeds.
3. Mix dressing ingredients together in a jar.
4. Place carrots in a bowl, massage briefly with a dash of umeboshi vinegar, and set aside.
5. Bring 8 cups of water to a boil in a large pot. Blanch each vegetable individually and set aside to cool.
6. In the same water, cook noodles according to the directions on the package. Rinse under cold water and drain. Set aside.

TO ASSEMBLE THE SOBA SALAD:

1. Place fresh lettuce leaves on a plate.
2. Place soba noodles in the center of the lettuce.
3. Place blanched vegetables, tempeh, carrots, cucumbers, and roasted peppers, if using, on top of the noodles, lined up nicely in a row next to one another.
4. Top with scallions for garnish, and serve with dressing drizzled on top.

CHEF'S TIP: *Any seasonal vegetables and leftovers may be utilized for this salad. It's a great way to use up extra vegetables from your refrigerator.*

PAD THAI WITH TEMPEH

SERVES 3–4

Here is a healthy and tasty vegan pad Thai recipe. The tropical flavors of the sweet & sour noodles, the vegetables, and the nutty peanut topping contribute to its worldwide popularity. Often pad Thai is made with refined sugar; instead, this recipe calls for brown rice syrup for a healthier dish!

PAD THAI SAUCE

¼ cup fresh lime juice

2 tablespoons brown rice syrup

2 tablespoons shoyu or tamari

⅛–¼ teaspoon red chili flakes (optional)

PAD THAI

3 tablespoons sesame oil, divided

4 ounces tempeh, cubed

6 ounces pad Thai rice noodles

1 cup sliced onion (thin half-moons)

few pinches of sea salt

1 clove garlic, minced

½ cup sliced carrots (thin matchsticks)

4 ounces (about 1 handful) mung bean sprouts

GARNISH OR TOPPING

⅓ cup fresh cilantro

¼ cup chopped green onions (thin diagonals)

¼ cup lightly crushed roasted peanuts

lime wedges

1. In a small saucepan, combine the sauce ingredients, stirring thoroughly, and bring to a boil. Simmer for 5 minutes, then set aside.

2. Heat 2 tablespoons of oil in a skillet over a medium flame. Add tempeh and fry until golden brown. Set aside.

3. In a large saucepan, bring 5 cups of water to a boil. Remove from flame. Add rice noodles, stir, and let stand 8–10 minutes or until noodles are soft but firm. Drain well and rinse under cold water. Set aside.

4. Heat 1 tablespoon of oil in a skillet over a medium-high flame. Add onion, sea salt, and garlic, and stir for 4–5 minutes until onion becomes translucent. Add carrots and stir for 3–4 minutes.

5. Add tempeh cubes and continue to sauté for a few more minutes.

6. Slowly pour pad Thai sauce over skillet. Then add noodles on top. Stir gently until thoroughly mixed.

7. Remove from flame and add bean sprouts, tossing gently to combine.

8. Pour onto a platter and garnish with cilantro, green onions, and crushed peanuts.

9. Serve immediately with lime wedges.

NOODLE SUSHI ROLLS

MAKES 4 ROLLS

Sushi is usually made with rice, but it can also be made with noodles. This tasty variety includes soba or udon rolled in nori with cucumber, carrots, sauerkraut, and string beans. The wasabi dipping sauce adds a hot, pungent taste to this elegant dish.

SUSHI ROLLS

6 ounces noodles (soba, somen, or udon)

4 sheets sushi nori

1 medium cucumber, seeded and sliced into long pieces

2 medium carrots, shredded

4 tablespoons sauerkraut

1 cup blanched string beans

WASABI DIPPING SAUCE

¼ cup water

1 tablespoon shoyu

1 teaspoon wasabi powder

TO MAKE THE SUSHI ROLLS:

1. Cook noodles according to the directions on the package. Rinse under cold water and drain.

2. Place a sheet of nori, smooth-side down, on a bamboo sushi mat.

3. Spread cooked noodles on the sheet of nori lengthwise, leaving ½ inch at the bottom of the sheet and 2½ inches at the top of the sheet uncovered.

4. Place vegetable ingredients lengthwise, in the center on top of the noodles.

5. Roll forward, pressing the sushi mat with your thumbs and tucking the nori over the noodles with your fingers. Continue to roll the nori sheet tightly around the noodles and stuffing. When the roll is almost completely rolled, moisten the far end of the nori with a little cold water. Wrap the whole roll in the sushi mat, and squeeze gently to seal the roll. Remove the mat from the sushi roll.

6. Place a small amount of cold water in a bowl. Place a nori roll on a cutting board. Dip knife into cold water. Slice roll in half, then slice each half in half, and then each quarter in half. You should now have eight pieces of noodle sushi. Arrange on a serving platter.

7. Repeat the above steps until all rolls have been sliced and the sushi has been arranged on the serving platter.

TO MAKE THE DIPPING SAUCE:

1. To prepare the dipping sauce, heat up water, season with shoyu, and simmer without boiling for 3 minutes.

2. Turn off flame and allow to cool.

3. Add wasabi powder and mix.

FRESH SPRING ROLLS WITH PEANUT SAUCE

MAKES 7–8 SPRING ROLLS

Everyone loves these fresh, tasty Vietnamese-style spring rolls. These rainbow-colored spring rolls are filled with flavorful ingredients: fresh vegetables, herbs, rice noodles, and fried tofu. When the refreshing herby flavor meets the rich fried tofu and the creamy, sweet, and savory peanut sauce, you find yourself in paradise, happily devouring every single bite.

SPRING ROLLS

3 ounces thin rice noodles or Asian vermicelli

half a (14-ounce) package tofu, drained and pressed for 30 minutes, then sliced into strips

7–8 rice spring roll papers

3 cups fresh curly or butter lettuce, washed and dried in a salad spinner

1 cup sliced cucumber (thin matchsticks)

1 cup sliced carrots (thin matchsticks)

1 cup shredded red cabbage, marinated with ½ teaspoon umeboshi vinegar for 10 minutes

½ cup alfalfa or broccoli sprouts

¼ cup fresh whole cilantro leaves, stems removed

¼ cup fresh whole mint leaves, stems removed

PEANUT BUTTER DIPPING SAUCE

¼ cup peanut butter

1 tablespoon lime juice

1 tablespoon shoyu

½ tablespoon rice syrup

1 teaspoon umeboshi vinegar

pinch of chili flakes (optional)

TO MAKE THE SPRING ROLLS:

1. Cook rice noodles in boiling water for 5–10 minutes according to the directions on the package. Drain, rinse with cold water, and set aside.

2. Meanwhile, deep-fry tofu strips until golden. Set aside on a paper towel to cool and drain excess oil.

3. To assemble spring rolls, prepare warm water in a shallow dish and immerse one sheet of rice paper at a time for 5–10 seconds to soften it (some rice paper is thicker and needs longer time in the water to soften, so check the instructions on the package).

4. Transfer rice paper to a damp cutting board.

5. Place lettuce in the center of the rice paper. Then add layers: rice noodles, cucumber, carrots, red cabbage, sprouts, and a piece of fried tofu. Top with a little cilantro and mint. Don't put too much filling in the spring roll, as it may be difficult to seal.

6. Starting with the edge closest to you, gently fold the rice paper around the filling once, securely tuck the edges in on each side, and roll until it seals completely.

7. Place seam-side down on a serving plate and cover with a damp cotton cloth to prevent the rolls from drying out.

8. Repeat until all the filling runs out. This makes about 8 rolls.
9. Serve with peanut sauce. Best served fresh.

TO MAKE THE DIPPING SAUCE:

1. In a medium suribachi or mortar, combine the dipping sauce ingredients.
2. Using a surikogi or a pestle, mix well. Slowly add warm water until sauce reaches the desired consistency (usually about 3 tablespoons). Adjust flavor if needed.

GYOZA DUMPLINGS

MAKES 2–5 DUMPLINGS

Gyoza is a Japanese version of Chinese dumplings, or *jiaozi*. This plant-based gyoza is stuffed with vegetables and mushrooms. The simple pan-fried dumplings are absolutely delightful!

2 tablespoons sesame oil, divided

1 cup finely diced onion

several pinches of sea salt

1 teaspoon minced garlic

1 teaspoon minced ginger

4 fresh shiitake mushrooms, finely chopped (about 1 cup)

3 cups finely chopped cabbage

¼ cup finely chopped scallions

white pepper, for sprinkling (optional)

gyoza wrappers

DIPPING SAUCE

2 tablespoons brown rice vinegar

1 teaspoon hot sesame oil (optional)

1½ tablespoons shoyu

TO MAKE THE FILLING:

1. Heat 1 tablespoon of the sesame oil in a skillet and sauté onion with a few pinches of sea salt until translucent.
2. Add garlic, ginger, and shiitake mushrooms, and continue to sauté with a few pinches of sea salt.
3. Add cabbage and a few more pinches of sea salt, as needed. Continue to sauté for 5 minutes until cabbage softens but remains crispy. Add scallions.
4. Sprinkle a little white pepper, if using, and continue to sauté for a few more minutes. Set aside to cool.

TO MAKE THE DUMPLINGS:

1. Place a gyoza wrapper on your palm and ladle about ½ tablespoon of the filling in the center.
2. Using your fingers, apply a little water along half of the edge.
3. Fold the wrapper over and seal securely, pressing down to create a pleated edge.
4. Repeat with each wrapper.

TO PAN-FRY THE GYOZA:

1. Heat a cast-iron skillet and add remaining 1 tablespoon of sesame oil.
2. Place the gyoza into the skillet in line formations, making sure to leave room between each row so that they may be easily flipped over with your spatula.
3. Pan-fry until the bottom of the gyoza is crispy and golden brown. Flip the gyoza over with a spatula.
4. Fry the side you just flipped onto in the skillet until it is a golden color. Remove from skillet and place on a serving plate.
5. Make dipping sauce by mixing ingredients well in a small bowl.
6. Serve gyoza hot with dipping sauce.

VARIATION | Instead of fresh shiitake mushrooms, you may use two dried shiitake. Soak them with water until soft and then chop finely. It is also nice to cook gyoza by deep-frying, steaming, or putting them in a soup.

CHEF'S TIP: *Uncooked gyoza can be refrigerated for one day. If you don't cook them within that time, gyoza can be frozen for up to a few weeks. Be sure to freeze them separately before packing them in a container or they will stick together.*

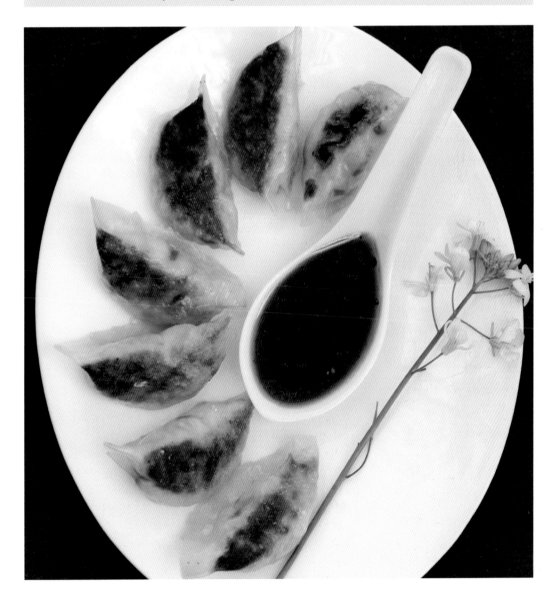

OKONOMIYAKI (SAVORY JAPANESE PANCAKES)

MAKES 5–6 PANCAKES

Growing up in Japan, okonomiyaki was one of Sachi's favorite dishes from childhood, and she still adores it. Whenever she finds a *nagaimo* (Japanese mountain potato) in a store, she likes to include it in this pancake recipe. But if you can't find it, it is OK to leave it out.

BATTER

½ cup all-purpose flour

½ cup grated nagaimo (Japanese mountain potato) (optional)

⅓ cup SHIITAKE BROTH (page 98) or water

1 teaspoon mirin (optional)

dash of shoyu

⅛ head of cabbage, finely shredded (2 cups)

2 scallions, finely chopped

safflower oil, for pan-frying

SAUCE

3 tablespoons shoyu

1 tablespoon brown rice syrup

1 tablespoon sake or water

TOPPING

TOFU MAYONNAISE (page 226) (optional)

1. Place all the batter ingredients through shoyu in a mixing bowl. Mix gently until the texture becomes smooth. Put in refrigerator for 30 minutes.
2. While the batter is cooling, heat sauce ingredients briefly in a small pan and set aside.
3. Remove batter from refrigerator. Add cabbage and scallions to batter and mix harmoniously.
4. Heat oil in a cast-iron skillet over medium heat, and spoon batter into round shapes on the skillet (about ½ cup for each pancake).
5. Pan-fry both sides until golden brown.
6. Brush the sauce on top of the pancake and top with tofu mayonnaise.

MACRO CORN BREAD WITH TAHINI-MISO SPREAD

SERVES 8

This recipe is inspired by Angelica Kitchen, one of our favorite vegan restaurants in New York. This corn bread is wonderful with or without the tahini spread!

2 tablespoons toasted sesame seeds

½ cup fresh or frozen organic corn

3 cups cooked rice

WET

½ teaspoon sea salt

2 cups apple juice

3 tablespoons safflower oil

DRY

1 cup rolled oats

⅓ cup polenta

1 cup cornmeal

TAHINI-MISO SPREAD

1⅓ cups tahini

⅓ cup sweet miso (white or chickpea miso)

1. Preheat oven to 350°F. Oil or place a parchment paper on a 8 × 5 × 3 loaf pan or 8 × 8 square baking pan. Sprinkle sesame seeds evenly on the bottom of the pan.

2. In a mixing bowl, mix wet ingredients until well blended.

3. Place dry ingredients in a large mixing bowl, pour the wet mixture on top, and stir together. Add corn and cooked rice, and stir everything well.

4. Pour mixture into the prepared baking pan. Bake for 40–45 minutes or until firm and the color turns golden.

5. Meanwhile, make tahini-miso spread by blending tahini and sweet miso in a food processor. Add ½ cup of water little by little until texture becomes smooth.

6. Serve sliced corn bread with spread over the bread or served on the side.

"Bread I at first made of pure Indian meal and salt, genuine hoecakes, which I baked before my fire out of doors on a shingle or the end of a stick of timber sawed off in building my house."

—Henry David Thoreau, *Walden*

FRENCH TOAST

SERVES **4–5**

This healthy French toast is a dream come true. French toast is a favorite treat for those brought up eating eggs and dairy. This vegan version is as delicious as classic French toast or even better!

BATTER

1 cup firm tofu (Mori-Nu Firm Tofu works really well)

1 cup soy milk or almond milk

1 tablespoon safflower oil

2 tablespoons maple syrup

1 teaspoon vanilla extract

1 teaspoon cinnamon powder

⅛ teaspoon sea salt

⅛ teaspoon turmeric powder (optional, for bright yellow color)

FRENCH TOAST

8–10 slices sourdough bread

safflower oil, for pan-frying

fresh fruits or fruit compote, for topping

maple syrup, for topping (optional)

1. Place all the batter ingredients in a food processor and blend together until smooth and creamy. If the batter is too thick, add a little more milk.

2. Dip each sourdough bread slice in the batter. You only need to dip each side quickly. If you dip the bread slices too long in the batter, it results in soggy French toast.

3. Heat a little oil in a frying pan, and fry each slice until browned on both sides.

4. Serve with fresh fruits or fruit compote. If you like, drizzle some maple syrup on top.

Corn Chowder
(see recipe on page 107)

MISO SOUP AND OTHER APPETIZING SOUPS

"Between soup and love, the first is better."
—OLD SPANISH PROVERB

KOMBU AND SHIITAKE BROTH

MAKES 3 CUPS

Kombu and shiitake broth, known as dashi, is the basis for many soups, stews, and dishes. Alternatively, just kombu or shiitake broth may be served—see variations.

3-inch square piece kombu

1–2 dried shiitake
    mushrooms

TO MAKE THE BROTH BY SOAKING:

1. Place kombu and shiitake mushrooms in a jar.
2. Soak with 3 cups of water overnight, up to 24 hours, in the refrigerator before using.

TO MAKE THE BROTH BY SIMMERING:

1. In a saucepan, place 3 cups of water, kombu, and shiitake mushrooms. Soak kombu and shiitake in the water for 10 to preferably 30 minutes.
2. Simmer over a medium-low flame.
3. Just before broth comes to a boil, take out kombu.
4. Continue to simmer shiitake mushrooms for 10–30 more minutes.

VARIATIONS | To make **Kombu Broth**, a lighter alternative, omit shiitake and follow the instructions above. To make **Shiitake Broth**, omit kombu and follow the instructions above.

VEGETABLE BROTH

MAKES 4 CUPS

Vegetable scraps make great broth. Instead of throwing scraps away, we can turn them into broth to make rich, flavorful soups and stews.

2 cups vegetable scraps
    (such as onion skins
    and ends, winter squash
    skins, roots of leeks,
    etc.)

1. Place vegetable scraps and 4 cups of water in a pot and bring to a boil over a medium flame.
2. Cover, reduce flame to low, and simmer for 40 minutes.
3. Pour the broth through a fine mesh strainer over a heatproof container. Discard the vegetable scraps.
4. Once broth has cooled, keep in fridge for up to 3–4 days.

MISO SOUP

SERVES **4-5** *(see photo on page viii)*

The vitamins, minerals, and probiotics in miso strengthen the intestines as well as purify the blood. Having a bowl of miso soup at breakfast is a great way to start off the day.

4-inch piece wakame, rinsed and soaked in ½ cup of water until soft, and finely diced

1–2 dried shiitake mushrooms, soaked with 1 cup water until soft, and finely sliced; reserve soaking water

½ cup sliced yellow onion (thin half-moons)

¼ cup thinly sliced carrots

½ cup finely sliced leafy vegetables (bok choy, collard greens, kale, etc.)

5 teaspoons miso paste, or to taste

scallions, for garnish

1. In a saucepan, combine 3 cups of water, wakame, shiitake, and the shiitake soaking water, and bring to a boil.
2. Add remaining vegetables except leafy greens and return to a boil. Reduce flame to medium-low and cook until vegetables are soft, about 10 minutes.
3. Add leafy greens and cook until the color turns bright green.
4. Reduce flame to low. Remove a small amount of broth, use to dissolve miso in a small bowl, and stir gently back into the broth.
5. Simmer, uncovered, for 3–4 minutes to activate the enzymes. After adding miso, never boil the broth, to preserve the enzymes.
6. Serve with garnish.

CHEF'S TIP: *You can make miso soup all year round by adding seasonal ingredients. For example: springtime sprouts and celery, summertime corn kernels, autumn kabocha squash, and winter-time root vegetables, such as burdock root.*

You can choose the type of miso according to the seasons or your needs. Use a lighter color and mellow miso for warmer seasons and to relax. Use a darker miso or long-aged miso for colder seasons and to strengthen or heal.

Lighter color mellow miso pastes:
white miso, chickpea miso, mellow barley miso

Darker color aged miso pastes:
1- or 2-year aged barley miso, brown rice miso, hatcho (all soybean) red miso

MISO SOUP AND OTHER APPETIZING SOUPS   99

CREAMY KABOCHA SOUP

SERVES 4–5

Puréed squash soup provides satisfying sweetness, and the creamy texture is very relaxing. Fall- or winter-season squash is especially nourishing to the central organs like the stomach, pancreas, and spleen.

2 teaspoons sesame oil

1 medium onion, diced

few pinches of sea salt, plus more to taste

4–5 cups chopped fall or winter squash (kabocha, buttercup, butternut, etc.) (large cubes)

parsley, for garnish

1. Heat oil in a heavy pot and sauté onion with a few pinches of sea salt until tender.
2. Place squash on top and add just enough water to cover the squash. Bring to a boil over a medium flame. Cover and reduce flame to low. Simmer for 20 minutes or until squash becomes tender.
3. Purée squash with an immersion blender until the texture becomes smooth and creamy.
4. Place the pot back on the medium flame, and season with sea salt to taste. Bring back to a boil, lower flame to low, and simmer for 10 minutes.
5. Garnish with parsley and serve.

CHEF'S TIP: *If you are using kabocha squash and want to preserve the bright orange color of the soup, the squash skin can be peeled. Save the skin for making soup stock. White miso can also be used for seasoning to give this soup a nice mellow taste.*

Tasty Kabocha

Selecting a good kabocha at the market is an art, and it comes down to finding a sweet specimen. To pick a good one, look for a dense and weighty kabocha squash with a relatively small and contracted navel. Another indicator of sweetness in a kabocha is a yellow or dark orange tint.

CELERIAC AND APPLE BISQUE

SERVES 4–5

This French-style soup made with celeriac has an amazing natural sweetness, and the creamy texture is absolutely delightful in the winter season. A hint of fennel seeds will brighten up the aroma and the natural sweetness of the celeriac.

1 tablespoon olive oil

1 small onion, diced (about ½ cup)

1 stalk celery, diced

few pinches of sea salt, plus more to taste

½ bulb celeriac, diced into bite-size pieces (about 2 cups)

1 apple (Gala or other sweet type), cored and diced into bite-size pieces

½ teaspoon fennel seeds

2 cups VEGETABLE BROTH (page 98) or water

black pepper

celery leaves, for garnish

1. Heat oil in a pan. Add onion and celery with a few pinches of sea salt and sauté until vegetables become soft, about 10 minutes.

2. Add celeriac and apple, and sprinkle ¼ teaspoon sea salt and fennel seeds. Then cover with a lid and cook for 10 minutes over a medium-low flame.

3. Add vegetable broth or water and bring to a boil. Cover and simmer for 20–30 minutes until all the celeriac become tender.

4. Remove from flame, and blend with a handheld immersion blender until smooth. Place the pot back on the stove over low flame, season with sea salt and black pepper, and simmer for 5 minutes.

5. Serve with garnish.

CHEF'S TIP: *It is preferable to use an enamel-coated cast-iron pan with a heavy lid. As with many soups, this heat-induction pot enhances the flavor and taste.*

CARROT-GINGER SOUP

SERVES 4–5

This soup makes a satisfying winter lunch or dinner. The gingery flavor warms you right up and is very relaxing.

1 tablespoon sesame oil or olive oil

1 cup diced onion

few pinches sea salt, plus more to taste

3 cups chopped carrots (roll-cut into bite-size pieces)

2 cups VEGETABLE BROTH (page 98) or water

2 teaspoons ginger juice

parsley, for garnish

1. Heat oil in a soup pot, and sauté onion until soft with a few pinches of sea salt. Add carrots, and continue to sauté for 5 minutes.

2. Pour vegetable broth or water to cover the vegetables, and bring to a boil. Cover, reduce flame to low, and simmer for 25–30 minutes or until vegetables become tender.

3. Blend soup with an immersion blender until the texture is creamy and place the pot back on a low flame. If the soup consistency is thick, adjust to desired thickness by adding some water. Season with sea salt to taste. Simmer for 5 minutes.

4. Add ginger juice, adjust the flavor, and simmer over a low flame for a few minutes to harmonize all the ingredients.

5. Serve with garnish.

CHEF'S TIP: *When you thoroughly sauté onions and carrots together in oil, the sweet flavor enriches the soup.*

CORN CHOWDER

SERVES 4–5

This soup is a summer delight. The creamy texture and the sweetness of the corn and vegetables make everyone smile.

1 teaspoon sesame oil

1 cup finely diced onion

¼ teaspoon sea salt, plus more to taste

½ cup finely diced celery

¼ cup finely diced carrots

½ cup finely diced cabbage

2 cups VEGETABLE BROTH (page 98) or water

3 cups fresh corn kernels (save corncobs for stock)

1 tablespoon white miso

parsley, for garnish

SOURDOUGH CROUTONS (page 187 from Caesar Salad), for topping (optional)

1. Heat oil in a medium soup pot over a medium flame and sauté onion with a few pinches of sea salt until the color turns translucent and the aroma sweet. Add celery, carrots, and cabbage. Continue to sauté for 10 minutes. Add vegetable broth or water and the corncobs.

2. Slowly bring to a boil over a medium flame. Add corn kernels. Reduce flame to low, cover, and simmer for 20 minutes. Take corn cobs out of the broth and discard.

3. Take out 1 cup of vegetable pulp from the broth. Set aside. Blend everything else with an immersion blender until the soup becomes a creamy purée.

4. Place vegetable pulp back into the pot. Season with white miso and sea salt. Simmer for 10 minutes.

5. Serve with parsley and croutons for topping.

CHEF'S TIP: *Corncobs add amazing sweetness to broth, as they do in this soup. So the next time you take the corn off the cob, don't throw out the cob; save it and use it to make broth.*

HOT & SOUR SOUP

SERVES 4–5

This Chinese-style hot and sour soup is thickened with kuzu and is very warming. You can make this soup milder by using black pepper instead of white pepper or by omitting pepper altogether.

1 teaspoon sesame oil

½ cup diced onion

few pinches of sea salt, plus more to taste

3 cups VEGETABLE BROTH (page 98) or water

5 small fresh shiitake mushrooms, sliced (1 cup)

½ cup sliced carrots (matchsticks)

⅔ cup tofu cubes

SEASONING

1½–2 tablespoons shoyu

1½–2 tablespoons brown rice vinegar

1 teaspoon mirin (optional)

2 tablespoons kuzu

dash of white pepper (optional)

scallions, for garnish

1. Heat oil in a saucepan over medium flame. Add onion and a few pinches of sea salt, and sauté until translucent. Add vegetable broth or water, sliced shiitake mushrooms, carrots, and bring to a boil. Cover, reduce flame to low, and simmer for 15 minutes.

2. When carrots become soft, add tofu and cook for 5 minutes. Add shoyu, brown rice vinegar, mirin, and sea salt to flavor the soup.

3. In a small mixing bowl, prepare kuzu by dissolving it with 2 tablespoons of cold water.

4. Slowly pour in the kuzu mixture, stirring gently until the soup thickens and the color turns clear. Add a dash of white pepper, and serve with scallions.

VARIATION | It is also nice to add 1 cup of mung bean sprouts when adding the tofu.

CREAMY WHITE BEAN SOUP

SERVES 5–6

This creamy bean soup is exceptionally rich and satisfying. It is nice to serve with
SOURDOUGH CROUTONS (page 187).

1 cup dried white beans, soaked with 3 cups water overnight

1-inch square piece kombu

2 cups SHIITAKE BROTH (page 98) or water, plus more if needed

½ cup diced celery

¼ cup diced winter squash

3 thinly sliced fresh shiitake mushrooms

1 tablespoon white miso or chickpea miso

few pinches of sea salt, plus more to taste

parsley, for garnish

SOURDOUGH CROUTONS (page 187), for topping (optional)

1. Drain and discard soaking water from beans.
2. Place beans, 3 cups of water, and kombu in a heavy pot. Bring to a boil. Skim off white foam as it appears on the surface. Cover and simmer for about 1 hour until beans are soft.
3. Add enough shiitake broth or water to make soup desired consistency. Add vegetables and mushrooms to the beans. Once it starts boiling again, cover, reduce flame to low, and simmer for 20 minutes until vegetables become tender.
4. In a small bowl, dissolve miso with a small amount of the cooking broth.
5. Flavor soup with miso and sea salt. Simmer for another 10 minutes.
6. Serve with garnish and top with sourdough croutons.

CHEF'S TIP: *White beans include lima beans, navy beans, cannellini beans, and great northern beans. If it's summer and organic fresh corn is available, fresh corn kernels make a sweet, tasty addition to this soup. Add the corncob to the broth to enrich the soup as well!*

MIXED BEAN SOUP WITH HAZELNUT PESTO

SERVES 4–5

This soup is very rich and satisfying. Pesto is easy to make and enhances cooked or leftover beans.

HAZELNUT PESTO

1 cup hazelnuts

1 cup fresh basil leaves

5 tablespoons extra-virgin olive oil, plus more for storing

1 clove garlic, minced

½ teaspoon sea salt

BEAN SOUP

1 cup thinly sliced leeks

¼ cup diced carrots

¼ cup diced celery

1 medium potato, diced (optional)

1 small tomato, diced (optional)

2 cups VEGETABLE BROTH (page 98) or water

1 cup cooked white beans

1 cup cooked kidney or pinto beans

2–3 tablespoons pesto

sea salt, to taste

parsley or bean sprouts (broccoli or alfalfa), for garnish

TO MAKE THE PESTO:

1. Heat a skillet and dry roast the hazelnuts until their color turns golden brown.
2. In a food processor, grind hazelnuts into fine crumbles.
3. Add the rest of the ingredients and grind together until the texture becomes smooth and pasty. Adjust flavor if needed.
4. Put in a jar and add olive oil on top to preserve the bright pesto color. Store in the refrigerator for up to 1 week.

TO MAKE THE SOUP:

1. Add vegetables and broth or water to a saucepan. Over a medium flame, bring to a boil, cover, and simmer for 15–20 minutes until vegetables become soft.
2. Add cooked beans and bring back to a boil. Simmer for about 10 minutes until all the ingredients harmonize together.
3. In a small bowl, grind pesto into a smooth texture with some broth from the soup. Add to soup, and adjust flavor by adding sea salt; simmer for 10 minutes.
4. Serve with garnish.

> **CHEF'S TIP:** *You can use other leftover beans in this soup. Summer squash, green beans, and corn kernels are also very tasty in this recipe. Adding a handful of shell or elbow pasta makes a delicious pasta soup. For the pesto, you may use other kinds of nuts, such as pecans, walnuts, or pine nuts. Experiment!*

RED LENTIL DAHL

SERVES 4–5

This delicious dahl is one of our favorite summer soups. This beautiful bright-yellow soup is quite appetizing with its savory, tangy flavors and Indian spices. This would go well as a soup or served over rice or other grains.

RED LENTILS

1 cup red lentils, sorted and rinsed

1-inch square piece kombu

DAHL

2 tablespoons safflower oil

1 teaspoon cumin seeds

1 teaspoon brown mustard seeds

1 cup diced onion

1 teaspoon minced ginger

1 teaspoon minced garlic

¼–½ teaspoon sea salt, plus more to taste

1 teaspoon turmeric powder

1 bay leaf or curry leaf

2 tablespoons lemon juice

½–1 teaspoon umeboshi vinegar

cilantro leaves, for garnish

1. In a medium saucepan, combine red lentils, kombu, and 3 cups of water. Bring to a boil, skimming off the white foam as it arises on the surface. Cover the pot, reduce flame, and simmer for about 20 minutes or until the lentils become soft.

2. Heat oil in a medium soup pot. Add cumin and mustard seeds, and heat over a medium flame until they pop. Add onion, ginger, garlic, and sea salt, and stir for 5 minutes. Add turmeric powder and continue to stir until onion becomes translucent.

3. Add cooked lentils to the soup pot, adjust broth consistency by adding water to achieve desired thickness, and simmer with a bay leaf for about 10 minutes.

4. Adjust flavor with sea salt, and then finish by adding lemon juice and umeboshi vinegar.

5. Remove bay leaf and top with cilantro leaves for garnish.

FENNEL-POTATO SOUP

SERVES 4–5

This vegan version of potato soup is enticing for everyone. For a gourmet touch, top it with TEMPEH BACON (page 153) and enjoy!

SOUP

2 tablespoons olive oil

1 big fennel bulb, thinly sliced

½ teaspoon sea salt, or to taste

2 medium potatoes or sweet potatoes, cut into big cubes

1 clove garlic, minced

2 cups VEGETABLE BROTH (page 98) or water

black pepper (optional)

¼ cup soy milk or other nondairy milk (optional)

TOPPING

2 strips TEMPEH BACON (page 153), toasted lightly on a skillet and sliced into strips

fennel leaves, for garnish

1. Heat oil in a heavy pot over a medium flame and sauté fennel with sea salt for 4–5 minutes until the fennel turns translucent and the aroma sweet. Add potatoes, and continue to sauté for 5–7 minutes. Add vegetable broth or water, enough to cover the vegetables.

2. Bring to a boil over a medium flame. Cover, reduce flame to low, and simmer for 25–30 minutes until vegetables become tender.

3. Purée vegetables with an immersion blender until texture becomes smooth and creamy.

4. Place the pot back on the stove over a medium flame and bring back to a boil. Lower the flame to low and season with sea salt and black pepper, cover, and simmer for 10 minutes.

5. Keeping the flame low, pour in soy milk and simmer for a few minutes. Do not boil the soup.

6. Serve with toasted tempeh bacon strips and fennel leaves for garnish.

BORSCHT

SERVES 5–6

This Russian-style beet soup is adapted from a recipe from Maria Ivanov, Alex's daughter. The sunflower oil brings out the full flavor of the carrots and other vegetables. As served the Russian way, borscht is especially tasty topped with TOFU SOUR CREAM (page 227) and chopped dill.

2 cups chopped cabbage (bite-size pieces)

2 tablespoons sunflower oil

1 cup diced onion

½ cup diced celery

1 medium carrot, shredded (1 cup)

2 small beets, peeled and shredded (1½ cups)

½ teaspoon sea salt, divided

1 bay leaf

1 tablespoon tomato paste (optional)

1–2 teaspoons umeboshi vinegar

black pepper, to taste

TOFU SOUR CREAM (page 227), for topping

chopped dill, for garnish

1. In a heavy saucepan, combine cabbage and 3 cups of water, and bring to a boil. Cover, reduce flame to low, and simmer for about 15 minutes.

2. In the meantime, heat sunflower oil in a skillet. Sauté onion, celery, carrot, beets, and ¼ teaspoon of sea salt for about 10–15 minutes over a medium-low flame.

3. After vegetables turn tender, transfer to the saucepan, add remaining ¼ teaspoon of sea salt, bay leaf, and tomato paste, if using.

4. Slowly bring back to a boil, cover, reduce flame to low, and then simmer for 15 minutes. Add umeboshi vinegar and black pepper. Adjust taste if needed and simmer for 5 minutes.

5. Remove bay leaf and serve with tofu sour cream and chopped dill.

CHEF'S TIP: *Umeboshi vinegar has a great tangy taste, resembling tomato flavor. It is quite nice without tomato paste in case you want to avoid nightshades.*

Azuki Beans with Kabocha Squash
(see recipe on page 125)

RICH, SATISFYING BEANS

"Red Beans and Ricely Yours"
    —LOUIS ARMSTRONG'S SALUTATION AT THE END OF HIS LETTERS

"The grass of spring covers the prairies,
The bean bursts noiselessly through the mold in the garden,
. . . What chemistry!"

—WALT WHITMAN, "THIS COMPOST"

BEANS ARE TASTY, DELICIOUS, AND THE RICHEST PROTEIN SOURCE OF ALL DAILY foods. Soybeans contain nearly twice as much protein as beef. Plant-based protein is also easy to digest and does not contribute to cancer, kidney stones, or other chronic disorders associated with animal protein. The fiber in beans helps to bind and remove cholesterol from the body, protects the heart and circulatory system, and strengthens the intestines.

Beans are a natural complement to cereal grains. For millennia in the East, people traditionally ate soybeans and soy products such as miso, tofu, and tempeh with brown rice and millet. In India they ate lentils with whole wheat chapatis or rice. In the Middle East, they ate chickpeas and lentils with barley, wheat, and other grains. In the Americas, indigenous people ate black beans, pinto beans, and scarlet runner beans with maize.

In traditional Far Eastern medicine, beans are particularly strengthening for the kidneys, bladder, and reproductive system. Beans are also an excellent source of calcium, iron, and many other minerals and vitamins.

In the macrobiotic community, we serve beans daily and bean products such as tofu and tempeh several times a week (see chapter on Green Protein for these recipes). Major beans include:

Azuki Beans: Revered as an honorary grain in the Far East, azuki beans (also spelled *adzuki*) are flavorful small, oval-shaped red or brown beans that give strength and vitality and help protect against heart disease, cancer, diabetes, and other chronic disorders. Now grown and available worldwide, azuki beans are enjoyed as a tasty side dish, cooked with brown rice to make red rice, used in soup, or prepared with agar-agar, as in azuki *kanten*.

Chickpeas: Chickpeas are small, hard, compact beans that have an appetizing mild, sweet taste and give strong, soothing energy. In Spanish, chickpeas are called *garbanzos*. Chickpeas make a savory side dish or may be cooked with brown rice or other grains.

Lentils: Enjoyed worldwide for their nourishing and earthy taste, mild flavor, and soft texture, lentils are a traditional staple in India, the Middle East, southern Europe, and parts of South and Southeast Asia. Green lentils, the Middle Eastern type, are green to brown in color and red lentils, the Indian variety, range from orange to red. One popular variety is du Puy lentils. These are small blue-green marbled lentils grown in the volcanic soil of the southwest of France. Lentils make a satisfying soup by themselves or cooked with barley or other grains.

Soybeans: Containing the highest amount of protein of any food, including meat and dairy products, soybeans or soy products are the main protein sources for billions of people.

Soybeans, especially the black variety, are good for relaxing, softening, and warming the body. They are also especially good for female reproductive conditions. Originally from China and now grown around the world, soybeans may be cooked and eaten in whole form and have a mild, sweet flavor, but they are chiefly enjoyed processed into tofu, tempeh, shoyu, miso, *natto*, and other soy products.

Kidney Beans: Like other beans, kidney beans are delicious and high in protein, fiber, and other nutrients. They lower the amount of cholesterol in the body. They also keep blood sugar levels from rising too quickly and are recommended for people with diabetes. Also known as the chili bean, the large dark-red kidney bean resembles a kidney in shape. Native to many parts of the world, they are traditionally enjoyed in Central and South America, the Mississippi Delta, and in northern India, especially Punjab.

Pinto Beans: The most popular bean in the United States and northwestern Mexico, the pinto (or "painted") bean takes its name from its mottled beige skin with reddish-brown splashes of color. In addition to the nutritional benefits of other beans, pinto beans contain molybdenum, which protects against heart disease, cancer, diabetes, and other chronic disorders. When cooked, pinto beans turn pink and are enjoyed whole or mashed.

USES OF SOY AND SOY PRODUCTS

There is a large variety of soy products that can be used in different ways. Macrobiotics recommend miso and shoyu as suitable for daily use and for healing, in small amounts. Tofu, tempeh, *natto*, *kinako* (roasted soy powder), and whole soy beans themselves (especially black soy beans) can be used one to three times a week and are also suitable for healing in small amounts. We use commercial soy milk, soy nuts, and edamame infrequently for special occasions. Highly processed soy products, such as soy cheese, hot dogs, bacon, ice cream, textured soy protein, lecithin, and other soy supplements are best avoided.

Cooking Time for Beans

Beans may be boiled or pressure-cooked. Recommended cooking times for beans and use of seasoning are broadly listed in the accompanying chart. When preparing beans, please refer to the actual recipes as instructions for any given dish may vary slightly from this table.

COOKING TIME FOR BOILING BEANS			
TYPE OF BEANS	SOAKING TIME	ADD SEASONING	TOTAL COOKING TIME
SOFT BEANS brown and green lentils, red lentils, mung beans, and other soft beans	none (sometimes green lentils are hard and need 1–4 hours)	45–50 minutes	1 hour
MEDIUM BEANS French lentils, azuki, pinto, split peas, kidney, navy, lima, black, turtle, and other medium-size beans	4–8 hours	45 minutes to 1½ hours	2 hours
HARD BEANS chickpeas, black, white, and yellow soybeans, and other hard beans	6–8 hours, overnight, or up to 24 hours	3¼–3½ hours	4 hours

COOKING TIME FOR PRESSURE-COOKING BEANS			
TYPE OF BEANS	SOAKING TIME	ADD SEASONING	TOTAL COOKING TIME
SOFT	none	20–30 minutes	45 minutes
MEDIUM	4–6 hours or overnight	45 minutes	1 hour
HARD	6–8 hours or overnight	1–1½ hours	1½–2 hours

AZUKI BEANS WITH KABOCHA SQUASH

SERVES **4–5** *(see photo on page 120)*

This dish has a rich, sweet taste, balances blood sugar levels, nourishes the kidneys, and relaxes the pancreas and spleen. You may substitute butternut squash or other winter squashes if kabocha is unavailable.

1-inch square piece kombu

1 cup dried azuki beans, soaked with 3 cups water overnight, reserve soaking water

1½ cups diced kabocha squash

few pinches of sea salt

parsley, for garnish

1. Place kombu in a heavy pot and add azuki beans and bean soaking water. Bring to boil over a medium flame, skimming off white foam as it arises on the surface.
2. Reduce flame to medium-low, cover, and cook for about 45 minutes until beans become soft. Add water occasionally, as needed, but only just to cover the beans.
3. Add kabocha and sprinkle a few pinches of sea salt on top. Cover and continue to cook until kabocha becomes soft, about 20–30 minutes.
4. Mix everything gently, top with garnish, and serve.

CHEF'S TIP: *Do not mix this dish while it's cooking. This prevents beans from burning, as well as making the dish more harmonious and delicious.*

BLACK BEAN STEW

SERVES 4–5

This hearty dish is almost a meal in itself. It is tasty, filling, and energizing.

1 cup dried black turtle beans, sorted, washed, and soaked with 3 cups water overnight

1-inch square piece kombu

1 bay leaf

1 tablespoon sesame oil

1 clove garlic, minced

1 cup diced onion

¼ cup diced celery

¼ cup diced carrots

¼ cup fresh or frozen corn kernels

1 teaspoon cumin (optional)

sea salt, to taste

dash of shoyu

cilantro or parsley, for garnish

1. Drain beans, rinse, and discard soaking water. Place beans, kombu, and bay leaf in a heavy pot. Add water to cover 1 inch above the beans.

2. Slowly bring to a boil, skimming off white foam as it arises on the surface.

3. Place flame deflector underneath the pot, cover, reduce flame to medium-low, and simmer for 45 minutes or until beans become tender. If the liquid gets low during cooking, add some more water to cover the beans.

4. Heat oil in a skillet and sauté garlic, onion, celery, and carrots for a few minutes. Add sautéed vegetables to the bean pot.

5. Add corn, cumin, sea salt, and shoyu. Continue to simmer for 10 minutes until vegetables become tender.

6. Adjust the seasonings. Remove bay leaf and serve with garnish.

SWEET & SOUR BLACK-EYED PEAS

SERVES 4-5

This pea stew is inspired by Southern-style cuisine, of which black-eyed peas and other legumes are a traditional staple. The stew goes well with brown rice and MACRO CORN BREAD (page 93).

STEW

1 cup dried black-eyed peas, sorted, washed, and soaked with 3 cups water overnight

1-inch square piece kombu

1 cup diced onion

½ cup fresh or frozen corn kernels

½ cup green peas

SEASONINGS

1 tablespoon barley malt

1 tablespoon brown rice syrup

1 tablespoon brown rice vinegar

½ teaspoon umeboshi vinegar

2 teaspoons shoyu

⅛–¼ teaspoon sea salt, or to taste

parsley, for garnish

1. Drain black-eyed peas, rinse well, and discard the soaking water. Place kombu and peas in a heavy pot. Add water to cover 1 inch above the peas. Bring to a boil over a medium flame, skimming off white foam as it arises on the surface. Cover, reduce flame, and simmer for about 1 hour until peas become tender. As the liquid evaporates, add some more water to the pot to keep peas covered with liquid.

2. Add onion and seasonings. Cover and simmer another 10 minutes until onion turns tender and the flavors harmonize together in the pot.

3. Add corn and green peas, cover, and cook for 5 more minutes. Taste, adjusting flavor if necessary.

4. Serve with garnish.

VARIATION | Instead of umeboshi vinegar, use Dijon mustard. It also gives a nice, tangy flavor.

REFRIED PINTO BEANS

SERVES 4–5

This rich and creamy pinto bean recipe is absolutely everyone's favorite. It is nice to serve these refried beans alongside rice or with corn tortillas and top with TOFU SOUR CREAM (page 227) as a part of a healthy Mexican meal.

1 cup dried pinto beans, sorted, washed, and soaked with 3 cups water overnight

1-inch square piece kombu

1 cup diced onion

1 bay leaf

GARLIC SAUCE

1–2 cloves garlic, crushed

1 tablespoon extra-virgin olive oil

¼ teaspoon sea salt

sea salt, to taste

dash of shoyu or tamari (optional)

small amount chili powder (optional)

parsley or cilantro, for garnish

1. Drain beans, rinse, and discard soaking water. Place beans and kombu in a pressure cooker. Add water to cover 1 inch above the beans. Bring to a boil, skimming off the white foam as it arises on the surface. Close pressure cooker lid and bring up to pressure, reduce flame to medium-low, and cook for 45 minutes. Remove from flame, allowing pressure to come down.

2. Place pressure cooker pot over medium flame. Add onion and bay leaf, bring to a boil, cover with a heavy lid, reduce flame to medium-low, and simmer for 20 minutes until onions become soft.

3. While the beans and onion are cooking, make garlic sauce by mixing the ingredients in a suribachi or a bowl.

4. When onion becomes soft, mash half the portion of refried beans.

5. Add garlic sauce to beans and stir gently.

6. Season with sea salt and shoyu or tamari and chili powder, if using. Keep simmering for a couple of minutes.

7. Mix gently, remove bay leaf, and serve with garnish.

CHEF'S TIP: *Instead of pinto beans, you can also use other beans such as kidney beans and white beans. Beans rich in fat work well in this recipe.*

CHILI CON TEMPEH

SERVES 4–5

This vegan chili is so delicious that you'll have to do portion control! Chili is usually spicy, but for people who can't handle much heat, this recipe is only mildly spiced. Chili con Tempeh is a complete meal when served with brown rice, polenta, or a slice of corn bread. And of course, a dollop of TOFU SOUR CREAM (page 227) is a great topping.

1 cup dried chili beans or kidney beans, sorted, washed, and soaked with 3 cups water overnight

1-inch square piece kombu

3 tablespoons safflower oil

4 ounces tempeh, cut into 1-inch square cubes (1 cup)

1 cup diced onion

few pinches of sea salt, plus more to taste

1 clove garlic, minced

¼ cup tomato purée (optional)

½ cup fresh or frozen corn kernels

1–1½ tablespoons shoyu

SEASONINGS

1 teaspoon cumin powder

¼ teaspoon chili powder (optional)

¼ teaspoon smoked paprika (optional)

TOFU SOUR CREAM
(page 227), for topping

parsley or cilantro, for garnish

1. Drain beans, rinse well, and discard soaking water. Place beans and kombu in a pressure cooker. Add water to cover 1 inch above the beans. Bring to a boil, skimming off white foam as it arises on the surface. Close the pressure cooker lid, bring up to pressure, and cook for 45 minutes. Allow pressure to come down.

2. Heat 2 tablespoons of safflower oil in a small skillet and pan-fry tempeh cubes until golden. Mash tempeh cubes in a suribachi until they become small crumbles.

3. Heat 1 tablespoon of safflower oil in a pot and sauté onion with a few pinches of sea salt until translucent. Add garlic, tomato purée, if using, and seasonings.

4. Add beans together with the cooking liquid and tempeh crumbles. Bring back to a boil, reduce flame to low, and simmer for 10 minutes. If the stew gets dry, add water to keep the stewlike consistency. Cover and simmer for 10 minutes.

5. Add corn and shoyu and simmer for a few more minutes.

6. Taste chili and adjust flavor if necessary. Serve with tofu sour cream and garnish.

LENTIL BURGER

This scrumptious burger is a fave among plant-based burgers. It is inspired by the Plant Burger at The Plant restaurant in San Francisco. Sachi was so amazed by the sensational taste of this burger the first time she tried it that she just had to recreate it herself. The touch of beets turns the burgers a beautiful red and makes the plate colorful. It is nice to serve in a sourdough sandwich with Dijon mustard or alongside a fresh salad.

1 small beet, peeled and sliced into ½-inch lengths

several pinches of sea salt

½ cup bulgur wheat

1 tablespoon sesame oil, plus more for pan-frying

1 cup diced onion

1 cup sliced button mushrooms

¼ teaspoon cumin powder

¼ teaspoon dried thyme

⅓ cup cashew nuts

1½ cups cooked lentils (cooked from ½ cup dry lentils)

Dijon mustard, for topping

TO ROAST THE BEETS:

1. Preheat oven to 400°F.
2. Place beets on an oiled baking sheet and roast for 20 minutes until soft.
3. Set aside to cool.

TO MAKE BULGUR WHEAT:

1. In a small saucepan, bring ½ cup of water to a boil. Add a pinch of sea salt and the bulgur wheat and stir briefly with a whisk.
2. Cover, turn off flame, and let stand for 10 minutes. The bulgur should absorb the water and become tender.

TO MAKE VEGETABLE MIXTURE:

1. Heat 1 tablespoon of the oil in a skillet over medium flame and sauté onion with a few pinches of sea salt until translucent.
2. Add mushrooms, a few more pinches of sea salt, cumin powder, and thyme, and continue to sauté until onion and mushrooms become soft. Set aside.

TO MAKE BURGER PATTIES:

1. Place cashew nuts in a food processor and pulse until the texture becomes powdery.
2. Add roasted beets, cooked lentils, bulgur, and vegetable mixture. Pulse to combine everything. Add a little sea salt to taste, if needed. Process until mixture becomes pasty but not entirely smooth, leaving some cashew nuts coarse to keep the mixture slightly crunchy in texture.

3. Form mixture into patties by hand, making 5–6 oval patties.
4. Heat a little sesame oil in a skillet over medium flame and pan-fry each side of the patties until golden and crispy on the surface.
5. Top with Dijon mustard and serve in a sandwich or alongside fresh salad.

MOROCCAN RED LENTIL STEW WITH COUSCOUS

SERVES 4–5

This golden-colored lentil stew is appetizing, even intoxicating, with spices! It is perfect to serve with couscous or a slice of whole wheat sourdough bread.

STEW

1 cup red lentils

1-inch square piece kombu

2 tablespoons safflower oil

½ teaspoon minced ginger

1 cup diced onion

few pinches of sea salt

1–2 cloves garlic, minced

½ teaspoon cumin powder

½ teaspoon coriander powder

½ teaspoon turmeric powder

¼ teaspoon cinnamon powder

½ cup diced carrots

1½ cups diced butternut squash

1 cup cauliflower florets

1 bay leaf

2 tablespoons lemon juice

parsley, for garnish

COUSCOUS

pinch of sea salt

1 tablespoon olive oil

1 cup whole wheat couscous

1 tablespoon lemon zest

TO MAKE THE STEW:

1. Wash red lentils and place in a medium saucepan with kombu and 2 cups of water. Bring to a boil, skimming off the foam as it arises on the surface. Cover saucepan, reduce flame to low, and cook for about 20 minutes until lentils become soft. Set aside.

2. In the meantime, heat oil in a heavy pot, add ginger, and sauté for 3 minutes. Add onion, a few pinches of sea salt, garlic, cumin, coriander, turmeric, and cinnamon. Continue to sauté for about 5 minutes until onion becomes soft.

3. Add carrots, butternut squash, and cauliflower and continue to sauté for 2 minutes.

4. Add enough water to cover the vegetables and bring to a boil. Add bay leaf, cover, and simmer for 15–20 minutes until vegetables are soft.

5. Add cooked lentils to the vegetables and stew together for 10 minutes.

6. Season with sea salt to taste and continue to simmer for 5 minutes. Add lemon juice and mix gently.

TO MAKE THE COUSCOUS:

1. In a saucepan, bring 1½ cups of water to a boil. Add a pinch of sea salt and olive oil.

2. Add couscous and stir.

3. Cover, remove from flame, and let stand for 10 minutes.

4. Fluff the couscous and add lemon zest. Serve hot or at room temperature alongside stew with garnish.

FALAFEL WITH TAHINI-TOFU DRESSING

MAKES 15 FALAFEL BALLS

This falafel is less labor-intensive than you would think and absolutely delicious with tahini-tofu dressing or TAHINI DRESSING (page 192).

FALAFEL BALLS

1 cup dried chickpeas, sorted, washed, and soaked with 4 cups water overnight or preferably for 24 hours

¼ cup grated onion

1 teaspoon minced garlic

1 teaspoon coriander powder

1 teaspoon cumin powder

¼ teaspoon sea salt

safflower oil, for deep-frying

TAHINI-TOFU DRESSING

¼ cup TOFU MAYONNAISE (page 226)

¼ cup unsweetened soy milk or other nondairy milk

1 teaspoon tahini

sea salt, to taste

black pepper, to taste (optional)

1. Drain chickpeas, rinse well, and discard the soaking water.
2. Place chickpeas in a food processor and pulse coarsely.
3. Add onion, garlic, coriander, cumin, and sea salt, and continue to process until almost but not completely smooth.
4. Place the falafel mixture in a container and keep in a refrigerator overnight (preferably) or at least for a couple of hours, which prevents falafels from falling apart when deep-frying.
5. When ready to cook, form falafel balls and deep-fry them with safflower oil at 325°F until golden.
6. Mix ingredients for tahini-tofu dressing in a blender.
7. Serve falafel balls drizzled with tahini-tofu dressing in pita bread or a tortilla.

CHICKPEA CROQUETTES

SERVES 5–7

The sweet crunchiness of the deep-fried croquettes and the tangy sourness of the TOFU TARTAR SAUCE (page 226) make for a deeply satisfying combination.

1 cup dried chickpeas, sorted, washed, and soaked with 3 cups water overnight

1-inch square piece kombu

1 tablespoon olive oil or sesame oil

1 cup diced onion

¼ teaspoon sea salt, plus more to taste

1 clove garlic (optional)

⅔ cup diced brown mushrooms

½ cup finely diced carrots

½ cup fresh or frozen corn kernels

2 tablespoons minced parsley

⅓ cup pastry flour, plus more for coating

breadcrumbs, for dredging

safflower oil, for deep-frying

TOFU TARTAR SAUCE (page 226)

lemon slices, for garnish

1. Drain beans, rinse, and discard soaking water. Place beans in a pressure cooker and add enough water to cover 1 inch above beans.

2. Add kombu and bring to a boil, skimming off white foam as it arises on the surface.

3. Close the pressure cooker lid and bring up to pressure. Reduce flame and cook for 40 minutes.

4. Let pressure come down naturally. Open the lid and drain the liquid. Place chickpeas in a mixing bowl and allow to cool down for a while.

5. Meanwhile, heat olive or sesame oil in a skillet, and sauté onion with a few pinches of sea salt until translucent.

6. Add garlic, mushrooms, and carrots, and continue to sauté for about 5 minutes. Add corn kernels, season with ¼ teaspoon sea salt, and sauté for a few more minutes. Set aside.

7. Mash the chickpeas roughly using a potato masher. Add the vegetable mixture and minced parsley. Mix everything gently with a spatula.

8. Using your hands, shape mixture into 5 to 7 oval croquettes.

9. Roll each croquette in pastry flour to lightly coat all surfaces. Pat off excess flour.

10. Mix ⅓ cup of pastry flour with 6–7 tablespoons of water to make batter. Do not make it too thick.

11. Dip each croquette into batter briefly on both sides to make a thin coating, and then dredge in breadcrumbs, making sure the surface of the croquettes is completely covered. Repeat this process with each croquette.

12. Heat safflower oil in a heavy pot until hot, about 350°F. Deep-fry croquettes until the color turns golden and the texture is crispy.

13. Place croquettes on a paper towel to drain excess oil.

14. Serve with tartar sauce and a slice of lemon.

Autumn Fu Stew
(see recipe on page 147)

GREEN PROTEIN: TOFU, TEMPEH, SEITAN, AND FU

"From food are born all creatures, which live upon food and after death return to food. Food is the chief of all things. It is therefore said to be medicine for all diseases of the body."
—TAITTIRIYA UPANISHAD

HEALTHFUL PROTEIN IS GREEN, NOT RED. REAL PROTEIN COMES DIRECTLY FROM THE earth. It comes from plants. That's where most animals, such as beef and dairy cows, pigs, and chickens, get it in the first place. Whole wheat, oats, millet, and other whole grains are excellent sources of protein. Beans, nuts, and seeds are also rich repositories. Veggies, fruits, and other plant foods also contain modest amounts. Green protein is superior to red protein for daily health and vitality. Animal protein is harder on the kidneys, liver, and other organs, as well as body systems and functions than vegetable protein, and it comes with saturated fat (and often dietary cholesterol). Vegetable protein makes for a longer, happier life. And it's more economical and better for the planet, requiring only about 10 percent as much land and other resources to grow.

As Dr. T. Colin Campbell, director of the China Study and one of the world's leading nutritionists, warns, even "relatively small amounts of foods that are based on animal protein may be hazardous to your health." Meat, cheese, milk, eggs, and poultry weaken your bones, raise your cholesterol, and increase your risk for cancer.

Besides grains and beans, there are several high-protein foods that we use regularly. Tofu, tempeh, seitan, and fu are concentrated sources of highly accessible green protein that have traditionally been consumed for thousands of years in the Far East. Increasingly they are moving into the mainstream of modern society.

TOFU

Tofu originated in China millennia ago and reached Japan and other parts of the Far East as part of traditional Buddhist cooking known as *shojin ryori*.

The king of high-quality plant protein, tofu has a soft texture, mild taste, and versatile shape that combine well with many foods and absorb their flavors and aromas. It is enjoyed in soups, noodle dishes, casseroles, stir-fries, sandwiches, sauces, and spreads.

Tofu gives naturally cooling energy and is best eaten cooked. High in protein and oil, its natural balance is a salty or savory taste.

Once you open a package, tofu will keep for about three to four days in a covered glass container in the refrigerator. Keep the tofu covered with water, and change the water every day to prevent spoilage. Tofu is an excellent source of protein, calcium, iron, vitamin A, and B vitamins. It is very digestible and contributes to better circulation, respiration, and nerve functioning.

TEMPEH

Tempeh's rich, dynamic taste, firm texture, and strong meaty flavor make it a favorite. Made from fermented whole soybeans, tempeh also has one of the highest amounts of protein of any food and is easy to digest. The basis of delicious, satisfying soy protein burgers, cutlets, and stews, tempeh has circled the world from its native Indonesia to become a staple from Bali to Boston. Tempeh can be purchased ready-made, either plain or mixed with brown rice, millet, or other grain.

SEITAN

Seitan (also known as wheat meat or wheat gluten) is a dynamic, rich-tasting food popular in veggie burgers, stir-fries, cutlets, and other dishes. Made from wheat gluten cooked with shoyu and kombu, it is a staple of traditional Far Eastern cooking, especially among Buddhists who prefer a strong, high-energy vegetarian dish to animal-based food.

Seitan is high in protein, calcium, iron, and other nutrients, gives strength and energy, and contributes to general good health. It is particularly strengthening for the liver and gallbladder. Seitan can be purchased at natural markets.

FU

Fu is a soft wheat gluten product. With its light consistency, it absorbs liquid and expands when cooked. Fu is enjoyed added to soups and stews or cooked with vegetables. When fried, fu becomes a rich tasting, satisfying plant-based protein dish. Fu can be purchased online or at some Asian markets.

SHIRA-AE (JAPANESE TOFU SALAD)

SERVES 5–6

This tofu dip has a rich, nutty flavor, and the crunchiness of the vegetables melds with the creamy tofu texture to give it a great balance.

1½ tablespoons white miso

2 teaspoons tahini

1 (14-ounce) package firm tofu, cut into 6 square pieces, boiled for 10 minutes, and drained well

½ cup SIMPLE HIJIKI STEW (page 211)

¼ cup carrots (matchsticks), blanched and set aside to cool

1 cup leafy greens (such as mizuna, komatsuna, or kale), blanched and set aside to cool

1 tablespoon walnuts, roasted and coarsely crushed

⅛ teaspoon umeboshi vinegar

¼ teaspoon shoyu, or to taste

1 teaspoon lemon zest, for garnish

1. In a large suribachi or mixing bowl, place white miso and tahini and grind well with a surikogi.

2. Add boiled tofu and mash well until the texture becomes smooth.

3. Add hijiki stew, blanched vegetables, walnuts, umeboshi vinegar, and shoyu and mix well with a spatula. Taste, adjusting flavors if necessary.

4. Serve with garnish at room temperature or chilled in summertime.

AUTUMN FU STEW

SERVES **4–5** *(see photo on page 142)*

Kuruma-fu is a type of fu much larger than zeni-fu, with a rich, meaty texture.

SEASONING SAUCE

1½ tablespoons shoyu

1 tablespoon mirin

FU

4 pieces kuruma-fu, cut into halves

safflower oil, for deep-frying

STEW

1 tablespoon sesame oil

1 teaspoon minced ginger

2 cups diced onion

several pinches of sea salt

⅔ cup chopped winter squash (big chunks)

⅔ cup chopped sweet potato (big chunks)

½ cup sauerkraut

1 tablespoon sauerkraut juice

parsley, for garnish

1. Make seasoning sauce by mixing shoyu and mirin with ½ cup of water in a small bowl. Set aside.
2. Deep-fry fu in safflower oil until golden. Set aside to cool.
3. Heat sesame oil in a large skillet. Sauté ginger until it becomes light brown, add onion and a few pinches of sea salt, and sauté onion until translucent. Layer deep-fried fu, squash, and sweet potato on top of onion.
4. Pour seasoning sauce over the layers. Sprinkle a few pinches of sea salt on top. Cover, reduce flame to low, and simmer for about 20–30 minutes until squash and sweet potato become tender and the sauce is almost absorbed.
5. Place sauerkraut and sauerkraut juice on top and simmer for another 5 minutes.
6. Gently mix and serve with garnish.

TOFU QUICHE

This rich and hearty quiche is perfect for a special party menu or Sunday brunch.

CRUST

1½ cups pastry flour (unbleached white or whole wheat)

¼ teaspoon sea salt

4 tablespoons olive oil

SAUTÉED VEGETABLES

1 tablespoon olive oil

1 cup diced onion

few pinches of sea salt, plus more to taste

1 clove garlic, minced

2 cups thinly sliced mushrooms

¼ cup fresh or frozen green peas

¼ teaspoon thyme (optional)

TOFU MIXTURE

½ cup broccoli

1 (14-ounce) package tofu, pressed for 30 minutes

1 nagaimo (Japanese mountain potato, about 5 ounces), grated (optional)

1 tablespoon white miso

1 tablespoon umeboshi vinegar (½ tablespoon if not using nagaimo)

1 tablespoon arrowroot powder

¼ teaspoon turmeric powder (optional, for bright yellow color)

TO MAKE CRUST:

1. Preheat oven to 350°F. In a mixing bowl, combine flour and sea salt and whisk together.
2. Slowly add olive oil and mix with a fork. Then make crumbles by mixing with your hands.
3. Add ¼ cup of water, mix with hands, and make a round dough. If dough is still dry, add a little more water to improve its consistency.
4. Spread dough in a pie dish or tart mold.
5. Pierce with a fork to make tiny holes for air to escape during baking.
6. Bake for 10 minutes. Set aside to cool.

TO MAKE SAUTÉED VEGETABLES:

1. Heat oil in a skillet. Add onion and a few pinches of sea salt and sauté until translucent.
2. Add garlic, mushrooms, a few more pinches of sea salt, and continue to sauté for 3–4 minutes until mushrooms turn crispy.
3. Add green peas and thyme and sauté for a few more minutes. Set aside to cool.

TO MAKE TOFU MIXTURE:

1. Blanch broccoli and set aside in a separate bowl.
2. In a food processor, place the remaining tofu mixture ingredients. Process until texture is smooth. Taste, adjusting seasoning if necessary.

3. In a large mixing bowl, place tofu mixture, blanched broccoli, and sautéed vegetables. Mix thoroughly with a spatula.

TO BAKE TOFU QUICHE:

1. Heat oven to 350°F. Place tofu filling in the quiche crust and spread filling evenly.
2. Bake quiche for 30–40 minutes until the tofu filling sets and the surface turns golden.
3. Spread olive oil on the surface using a pastry brush to add shine to the surface before serving.

CHEF'S TIP: *You can omit* nagaimo *and reduce the umeboshi vinegar to ½ tablespoon. But if you can find* nagaimo, *it is nice to use in this dish. It creates a fluffy, almost egg-like texture for the quiche.*

MABO TOFU

SERVES 5–6

Mabo tofu, a tofu and vegetable stew with a gravy sauce, is one of the most popular home-cooked dishes in Japan. This recipe, inspired from a dish made by Sachi's grandmother, is recreated with a healthy touch and will be enjoyed by children and all ages. It is wonderful to serve with brown rice.

1 tablespoon sesame oil

½ tablespoon minced ginger

1 clove garlic, minced

½ cup finely chopped burdock root

few pinches of sea salt

1 cup diced onion

½ cup finely chopped shiitake or shimeji mushrooms

½ cup finely chopped lotus root

SEASONING SAUCE

1½ tablespoons barley or brown rice miso

1 tablespoon shoyu, plus more to taste

½ tablespoon mirin (optional)

dash of chili flakes (optional)

half a (14-ounce) package medium-firm or silken tofu, pressed for 15 minutes

1½ tablespoons kuzu, dissolved in 3 tablespoons cold water

scallions, for garnish

1. Heat oil in a skillet. Add ginger, garlic, burdock root, and a few pinches of sea salt and sauté for 3–4 minutes until the burdock aroma turns from woody to sweet.

2. Add onion, shiitake mushrooms, and lotus root and keep sautéing for 3–4 minutes until onion turns translucent.

3. In a small bowl, make seasoning sauce by mixing the ingredients together.

4. Add 2 cups of water, seasoning sauce, and a dash of chili flakes, if using, to the skillet, bring to a boil, and reduce flame to low. Cover and simmer for 20 minutes.

5. Cut pressed tofu into ½-inch cubes and add to skillet. Cover and simmer for 5 minutes.

6. Slowly add the dissolved kuzu, stirring gently until stew thickens.

7. Adjust flavor if necessary with shoyu and serve with garnish.

> **CHEF'S TIPS:** *Use milder seasoning and no chili flakes for children. It is also nice to use minced tempeh for children instead of burdock. They like its dynamic, enriched protein, and it helps keep up their energy level. If you use tempeh, add a little more oil when you pan-fry it in the beginning.*

SAVORY TEMPEH STRIPS

These savory tempeh strips are versatile. You can serve this tempeh in sushi rolls or on top of salads, such as the SOBA NOODLE SALAD (page 81).

MARINADE

½ cup apple juice

1 tablespoon shoyu

1 teaspoon brown rice vinegar

1–2 teaspoons sesame oil

1 teaspoon Dijon mustard

1 teaspoon mirin (optional)

1 teaspoon minced garlic (optional)

1 teaspoon minced ginger (optional)

dash of black pepper (optional)

8 ounces tempeh, cut into long ½-inch strips

1. Place all the ingredients of the marinade in a mixing bowl. Mix well with a whisk.

2. In a medium saucepan, place tempeh strips and then pour in the marinade.

3. Over a medium flame, bring to a boil. Cover the pot and reduce flame.

4. Simmer for about 20 minutes. Turn tempeh over after 5 minutes. Simmer tempeh until all the liquid is absorbed.

TEMPEH BACON

SERVES **4–5** (MAKES ABOUT **15–16** STRIPS)

This satisfying mock bacon tempeh tastes like the "real thing."

MARINADE

2 tablespoons apple juice

2 tablespoons olive oil

1 tablespoon apple cider vinegar

1 tablespoon maple syrup or brown rice syrup

2 tablespoons shoyu

1 teaspoon smoked paprika powder

1 teaspoon Dijon mustard

fresh ground black pepper, to taste

8 ounces tempeh, cut into ¼-inch strips

1. Preheat oven to 350°F.
2. Mix all the marinade ingredients together.
3. Place tempeh strips in a flat-bottomed casserole dish. Pour sauce over the tempeh strips and marinate for 10 minutes.
4. Bake marinated tempeh for 20–30 minutes until almost all the sauce is absorbed, flipping the tempeh strips after 10–15 minutes of baking.
5. Remove from the oven, let sit for 10–15 minutes, and serve.

SWEET & SOUR TEMPEH

SERVES **4–5**

This hearty stew blends tastes, flavors, and textures in delicious, uplifting harmony.

8 ounces tempeh, cut into bite-size triangles or squares

safflower oil, for deep-frying

1 tablespoon sesame oil

1 cup sliced onion (¼-inch quarter-moons)

¾ teaspoon sea salt, divided, plus more to taste

1 cup roll-cut burdock

½ cup sliced lotus roots (¼-inch half-moons)

½ cup roll-cut carrots

½ cup chopped cauliflower (bite-size florets)

2-inch square piece kombu

1 cup SHIITAKE BROTH (page 98) or water

½ cup apple juice

2 tablespoons brown rice syrup

2 tablespoons brown rice vinegar

2 tablespoons shoyu

2 tablespoons kuzu, dissolved in 3 tablespoons cold water

parsley or scallions, for garnish

1. Deep-fry tempeh pieces in heated safflower oil until golden. Set aside to cool.

2. In a skillet, heat sesame oil and sauté onion for a few minutes with ⅛ teaspoon of the sea salt until onion turns translucent.

3. Add burdock and ⅛ teaspoon of sea salt. Keep sautéing until burdock aroma turns from woody to sweet. Add lotus root, carrots, cauliflower, kombu, shiitake broth or water, apple juice, and ¼ teaspoon of sea salt. Bring to a boil, cover, reduce flame to low, and simmer for 20 minutes.

4. Add rice syrup, rice vinegar, shoyu, remaining ¼ teaspoon of sea salt, and fried tempeh. Cover and simmer for 10 minutes.

5. Taste broth and adjust flavor if necessary. Add dissolved kuzu while mixing gently until the broth thickens.

6. Simmer for another 5 minutes. Serve with garnish.

MINCED TEMPEH CUTLETS

SERVES 4–5 (MAKES 10–12 CUTLETS)

These delicious deep-fried cutlets are a big hit that the whole family will love.

16 ounces tempeh, cut into cubes

¾ cup apple juice

1 tablespoon shoyu

1-inch square piece kombu

2 tablespoons olive oil

½ cup finely diced onion

½ cup finely diced carrots

½ cup finely diced celery

¼ cup finely diced brown mushrooms

sea salt, to taste

¼ teaspoon cumin

⅛ teaspoon nutmeg

black pepper (optional)

2 tablespoons minced basil

2 tablespoons minced parsley

⅓ cup unbleached pastry flour

breadcrumbs, for dredging

safflower oil, for deep-frying

TOFU TARTAR SAUCE (page 226)

1. In a medium saucepan, place tempeh, ½ cup of water, apple juice, shoyu, and kombu. Bring to a boil, reduce flame, cover, and then simmer for about 20 minutes or until almost all the liquid evaporates.

2. Place tempeh in a big suribachi or mortar. With a surikogi, mash tempeh. Let cool.

3. Heat olive oil in a frying pan and sauté onion until translucent. Add carrots, celery, and mushrooms. Continue sautéing and lightly season with sea salt, cumin, nutmeg, and black pepper, if using.

4. Combine sautéed vegetables with mashed tempeh in the suribachi. Add basil and parsley. Mix well.

5. Shape mixture into round cutlets. Refrigerate for at least 2–3 hours or overnight, which will prevent them from falling apart when deep-fried.

6. Mix pastry flour with 6–7 tablespoons of cold water to make the batter.

7. Dip each cutlet in batter and then dredge cutlets in breadcrumbs.

8. Heat safflower oil to 350°F. Deep-fry each cutlet on both sides until golden.

9. Serve with TOFU TARTAR SAUCE.

SEITAN STROGANOFF

SERVES 4–5

This delectable, savory stew is especially popular among children. Rich in protein, it sustains energy and stamina and is ideal for people who engage in physical activity or who crave animal-based food. It is also warming and strengthening in cold weather. This creamy, saucy stew is perfect over noodles or rice topped with TOFU SOUR CREAM (page 227).

2 tablespoons sesame oil or olive oil, divided

1 (8-ounce) package seitan, sliced (1½ cups)

1 medium onion, cut into thin half-moons

2 cloves garlic, minced

½ teaspoon sea salt, divided

8 button mushrooms, thinly sliced

2 cups VEGETABLE BROTH (page 98) or water

1 tablespoon Dijon mustard

2 tablespoons almond butter

1½–2 tablespoons shoyu

1 tablespoon kuzu, dissolved in 3 tablespoons cold water

black pepper (optional)

½ cup blanched green peas, for topping

1. Heat a large skillet over medium-high flame. Add 1 tablespoon of oil and pan-fry both sides of the seitan slices until golden. Take out and set aside.

2. In the same skillet, heat remaining tablespoon of oil and sauté onion and garlic with ¼ teaspoon of sea salt until onion becomes translucent. Add mushrooms with a few pinches of sea salt, and sauté for 5–7 minutes.

3. Add vegetable broth or water and bring to a boil. Reduce flame to low. Add cooked seitan, mustard, almond butter, and shoyu. Cover and simmer for 15 minutes.

4. Taste, adjusting the flavor if necessary. Add dissolved kuzu and black pepper, if using. Stir until broth thickens. Simmer for a few minutes.

5. Serve stroganoff with blanched green peas over noodles or rice.

FU CUTLETS WITH APPLE-MISO SAUCE

SERVES 5–6

Zeni-fu is a small circular type of fu, named after the Japanese word *zeni*, meaning "coin." This savory fu cutlet is scrumptious and makes an enjoyable meal. The flavors of the fried cutlet and the miso sauce are from Sachi's hometown in Japan.

FU

20 zeni-fu (small rounds of fu)

1¼ cups KOMBU AND SHIITAKE BROTH (page 98)

1 tablespoon shoyu

1 tablespoon mirin

⅛ teaspoon sea salt

⅔ cup pastry flour, plus more for coating

panko (breadcrumbs), for dredging

safflower oil, for deep-frying

APPLE-MISO SAUCE

6 tablespoons red miso or aged dark barley miso

1 cup apple juice

4 teaspoons kuzu, dissolved in ½ cup apple juice

6 tablespoons finely chopped dill cucumber pickles

TO MAKE THE FU:

1. Soak zeni-fu in water for 15 minutes. When the fu pieces become soft, squeeze lightly without breaking them to remove excess water.

2. In a saucepan, place broth, shoyu, mirin, and sea salt and bring to a boil. Add zeni-fu, stacking in two or three layers. Make sure the liquid covers the zeni-fu. Cover and simmer for 15 minutes or until cooking liquid is absorbed into the fu. Set aside to cool to room temperature.

3. Squeeze fu lightly to remove excess liquid. Cover a surface with pastry flour and toss the fu to coat.

4. Combine ⅔ cup of pastry flour and ¾ cup of cold water in a mixing bowl and mix well to make batter. Dip fu into the batter and thinly coat each piece of fu.

5. Place panko in a mixing bowl. Coat each fu piece with panko evenly all around.

6. Heat safflower oil to 350°F. Deep-fry fu pieces until surface turns crispy and golden.

7. Serve with apple-miso sauce.

TO MAKE THE APPLE-MISO SAUCE:

1. Place miso in a small suribachi or mixing bowl. Slowly add apple juice while mixing with a surikogi to blend the paste into a smooth texture.

2. Place the miso mixture in a saucepan and warm up slowly to a gentle boil. Add dissolved kuzu and stir well for a few minutes until the sauce thickens.

3. Set aside to cool. Add dill cucumber pickles before serving.

Orange Baked Yams
(see recipe on page 175)

A CORNUCOPIA OF GARDEN VEGETABLES

"Foods that promote longevity, intelligence, strength, health, happiness and delight, which are sweet, nourishing, and agreeable, are dear to the Sattvic [balanced] type of people."
—BHAGAVAD GITA

VEGETABLES NATURALLY COMPLEMENT GRAINS AND BEANS. THERE IS A COLORFUL cornucopia of veggies to select from, while the number of grains and beans is limited. When people reduce animal-based food and become aware of the scope of the plant kingdom, their daily food palette expands rather than contracts.

For better health:

- Eat locally grown vegetables or veggies grown in a similar climate or environment
- Eat vegetables in season or pickled or dried naturally
- Eat at least one serving daily of leafy green vegetables, round or sweet vegetables, and root vegetables
- Eat about two-thirds of vegetables cooked. If desired, the rest may be eaten raw, lightly boiled, or lightly marinated in pressed salad
- Eat ecologically. For example, in a temperate climate, including most of North America and Europe, avoid vegetables of tropical or subtropical origin

THE ART OF CUTTING

Cutting is a Tao, or art, and macrobiotic cooks pride themselves on using the best vegetable knives and keeping them sharp. The standard knife for slicing vegetables is a large rectangular, wide-blade knife with a squared-off end and double bevel. It allows a flowing, back-and-forth motion that preserves the natural energy of the food. Mixing energies prior to cooking is largely avoided in the macrobiotic kitchen. Each vegetable is cut separately after rinsing the knife and kept on a separate plate until cooked.

There are innumerable ways to cut vegetables and other foods to enhance their taste, texture, and beauty. Each meal is a work of art, and the cutting methods employed will depend on the natural ki energy of the vegetable itself, the season and weather, the overall menu and balance of dishes prepared, the condition of the people you cook for, and the time available for cooking.

Thickly sliced vegetables take longer to cook than thinly sliced ones. They give stronger, more warming energy and are especially suitable for autumn or winter, while thinly sliced vegetables are more cooling and used more often in spring and summer. Even in the cooler seasons, however, we enjoy thinly sliced veggies, and in warmer seasons thicker ones. Only the proportions will differ. Leafy greens shrink in volume during cooking and do not keep their shape, while round and root veggies keep their shape and may be cut in many ways. If the ingredients in the soup are cut in large rounds, those in the main side dish may be diced, or vice versa. In preparing mixed vegetables, cutting each one in a different shape gives variety and uniqueness to the meal. The size of the pieces in one dish, however, should be relatively similar to ensure even cooking.

The ki energy of the food may also be enhanced by the style of cooking. Vertical cuts preserve the yin, or expansive, energy of the vegetable. Horizontal cuts create stronger, more yang energy. Cutting on the diagonal blends yin and yang and is often done to create balance and harmony.

In general, the knife should move in a forward motion across the vegetable you are cutting. The stroke should be smooth, fluid, and natural and will absorb the energy of your mind, body, and spirit as you cut. Don't saw, push, or hold the knife too rigidly.

There are thirteen major styles of cutting:

- **Rounds**—The vegetables are cut into thin or thick circular rounds.
- **Diagonal**—The vegetables are sliced on a slant by holding the knife at an angle. The angle of the blade determines the length of the pieces.
- **Half-Moons**—The vegetables are cut lengthwise into halves. Then each half is cut crosswise into thin rounds.
- **Quarters**—The vegetables are sliced lengthwise into halves. Then each half is cut down the center again. The four quarters are then sliced crosswise into small pieces.
- **Matchsticks**—Carrots, burdock, or other root vegetables are cut on the diagonal, sliced into thin matchsticks, and then cooked *kinpira* style.
- **Rolling or Irregular**—The vegetables are cut diagonally, rotating toward you 90 degrees after each cut. The pieces will be irregularly shaped but the same size.
- **Rectangles**—The vegetables are cut into large rounds one to two inches thick. Each round is then stood on its head and cut into four or five pieces, each piece one-fourth to one-third inch thick. Each section is then cut into thin rectangles.
- **Dicing**—The vegetables are cut into one- to two-inch chunks. Then each chunk is stood on end and cut into ¼- to ½-inch cubes by cutting vertically, then horizontally, and then crosswise. When dicing onions, cut the onion in half horizontally. Then cut thin parallel slices vertically, leaving the onion root attached. Then slice the opposite way toward the base. Finally, dice the root base into small pieces.
- **Mincing**—After dicing the vegetable, continue to chop very finely into small bits. Feed groups of dicings under the knife several times until only shavings remain.
- **Flower Shapes**—Cut four to five grooves around the vegetables lengthwise at equal distances. Then slice into thin rounds.
- **Shaving**—Root vegetables are shaved from the bottom like sharpening a pencil. Each vegetable is rotated slightly during shaving. The angle of the knife determines the thinness or thickness of the shavings.
- **Slicing Greens**—Two to three leaves are placed on top of each other. Then they are cut through the center along the spine of the leaves. Each halved leaf is then cut straight or on the diagonal into strips one-eighth to one-fourth inch thick. Finally, the spine is chopped very finely.
- **Whole**—Cooking a vegetable whole (without cutting) gives a unique, whole energy. Summer squash, carrots, onions, and other foods may occasionally be prepared in this way.

FRENCH STIR-FRY WITH MUSHROOMS AND PEAS

SERVES 4

This tasty French-style stir-fry combines sweet, sour, and pungent flavors and cooks up in just a few minutes.

STIR-FRY

1 tablespoon olive oil

½ cup diced onion

1 garlic clove, minced

1 cup sliced button mushrooms

few pinches of sea salt

¼ cup diced carrots

1 cup sliced sugar peas or frozen green peas

dill, for garnish

DRESSING

1 tablespoon lemon juice

1 teaspoon olive oil

1 teaspoon umeboshi vinegar

dash of black pepper (optional)

1. Heat olive oil in a large skillet.
2. Sauté onion and garlic until translucent. Add mushrooms and a few pinches of sea salt, stirring constantly. Add carrots and continue stirring for a few minutes. Add peas, stirring constantly for a minute.
3. Taste, adjusting flavor if necessary. Sauté for a few more minutes.
4. Transfer to a serving bowl. Mix the dressing ingredients. Pour over the stir-fried vegetables and serve with garnish.

KINPIRA

SERVES 4

Kinpira is Japanese for "golden pieces." Kinpira-style cooking involves cutting assorted root vegetables into matchsticks and sautéing and then simmering them to yield a crispy side dish with a nice savory flavor. This dish is very strengthening, especially for the intestines and reproductive organs.

1 tablespoon sesame oil

1 cup sliced burdock (matchsticks)

few pinches of sea salt

1 cup sliced lotus root (thin quarter-moons)

1 cup sliced carrots (matchsticks)

1 tablespoon shoyu, or to taste

2 teaspoons ginger juice (optional)

1 tablespoon toasted sesame seeds

1. Heat oil in a skillet over medium flame and sauté burdock for 3 minutes with a few pinches of sea salt until woody aroma turns sweet.

2. Add lotus root and carrots and sauté for 3 more minutes.

3. Lightly cover the bottom of the skillet with ½ inch of water. Bring to a boil, reduce flame to medium-low, cover the skillet, and simmer for 15–25 minutes until the vegetables are slightly tender and the water is almost absorbed.

4. Add shoyu and cover. Cook for a few minutes, uncover, and cook until almost all the liquid evaporates. At the end, add ginger juice, if using.

5. Add sesame seeds, mix gently, and serve.

VARIATIONS | For gluten-free *kinpira*, use tamari instead of shoyu. You can also substitute ingredients for this dish with other seasonal vegetables such as rutabagas, parsnips, onions, etc.

ROASTED VEGETABLES

SERVES 4–5

This hardy vegetable dish is strengthening, warming, and delicious, especially in late fall or winter. Vegetables can be varied depending on the season, and CILANTRO SAUCE (page 227) is great to serve with this dish.

1 cup roll-cut burdock (bite-size pieces)

1 cup roll-cut carrots (bite-size pieces)

1 cup chopped winter squash (bite-size pieces)

1 cup chopped cauliflower (bite-size florets)

1 cup sliced onion or fennel (big half-moons)

1 tablespoon olive oil

⅛ teaspoon sea salt

black pepper (optional)

1 tablespoon fresh or dried rosemary (if fresh, remove leaves from the stem and coarsely chop) (optional)

fresh herbs, chopped, for garnish

1. Heat oven to 400°F.
2. Mix vegetables in a large mixing bowl.
3. Toss with olive oil, sea salt, black pepper, if using, and rosemary, if using.
4. Transfer onto parchment paper on a baking sheet.
5. Roast vegetables in oven for 40 minutes to 1 hour. Check the vegetables every 10 minutes. Toss them around and bake until vegetables become tender.
6. Serve with garnish.

SAUTÉED DANDELION GREENS WITH MUSHROOMS AND CORN

SERVES 3–4

Dandelions are sometimes bitter to the taste, yet this way of preparation is delicious. By sautéing them with onions, the intense bitterness lessens, and the mushrooms enhance their umami flavor. The end result is a dish that is savory sweet with just a hint of natural bitterness. This is a great dish for cleansing the liver.

1 tablespoon sesame oil

1 cup sliced onion (thin half-moons)

1 clove garlic, minced

⅛ teaspoon sea salt

1 cup thinly sliced mushrooms

1 bunch dandelion greens, chopped in ½-inch lengths (about 3 cups)

1 teaspoon mirin (optional)

2 teaspoons shoyu

blanched corn kernels, for topping

1. Heat oil in a cast-iron skillet. Sauté onion and garlic with sea salt until onion becomes translucent. Add mushrooms and continue sautéing for 3–4 minutes until mushrooms are fully cooked.

2. Layer dandelion leaves on top with a little water added to the vegetables. Cover the skillet, lower flame, and steam for 1 minute.

3. Remove cover and sauté, stirring, until the dandelions turn a bright color. Taste and make sure the dandelions are sautéed until the bitterness becomes mild.

4. Season with mirin, if using, and shoyu. Taste, adjusting flavor if necessary.

5. Place blanched corn kernels on top and serve immediately.

SAUTÉED BROCCOLI RABE WITH MUSHROOMS

SERVES 4–5

Broccoli rabe is a delicious leafy vegetable with a slightly bitter flavor similar to broccolini or broccoli. It is especially flavorful when sautéed in oil. You may use broccoli or broccolini instead. This summer-style stir-fry is quick, easy, and divine!

1 tablespoon sesame oil

1 sliced onion (thin half-moons)

few pinches of sea salt

1 clove garlic, minced (optional)

2 cups thinly sliced mushrooms

1 bunch broccoli rabe, rinsed and cut into bite-size pieces, separating the leaf from the stem

2 teaspoons shoyu, or to taste

1. Heat oil in a skillet. Sauté onion with a few pinches of sea salt for 3–4 minutes. Add garlic and mushrooms and sauté for 2–3 minutes until they shine.

2. Add broccoli rabe stems, sauté for a minute, and then add the green parts on top.

3. Sprinkle a little water on the broccoli rabe, cover, and steam for 1–2 minutes on medium-low flame until the color of the greens turns bright. Remove cover and turn the flame up to medium. Sauté the vegetables for 1–2 minutes until the greens become tender.

4. Season with shoyu, stirring constantly, then serve.

VARIATION | Add tofu to turn this into a protein dish. Press the tofu cubes for 20 minutes to drain excess water before using.

ORANGE BAKED YAMS

SERVES **3–4** *(see photo on page 162)*

These orange-flavored baked yams are perfect for Thanksgiving dinner. Mixing different kinds of yams and sweet potatoes together makes for a unique taste and flavor.

4 cups chopped yams and sweet potatoes

1 tablespoon olive oil

1 tablespoon maple syrup

2 tablespoons orange juice

½ teaspoon cinnamon powder

¼ teaspoon ginger powder

¼ teaspoon sea salt

1 tablespoon orange zest, for topping

1. Preheat oven to 400°F.
2. Soak yams and sweet potatoes in water for 5 minutes and then drain well.
3. In a bowl, add olive oil, maple syrup, orange juice, spices, and sea salt to make the orange sauce. Add yams and sweet potatoes into the sauce bowl and mix well.
4. Place the mixture in a casserole dish and cover with foil. Bake for 30 minutes or until yams and sweet potatoes become tender. Remove foil and mix gently to coat yams and sweet potatoes with glaze.
5. Put back in the oven and bake for another 5-8 minutes.
6. Top with orange zest and serve.

FUROFUKI DAIKON

SERVES 3–4

This traditional Japanese dish helps clean deep inside the body, especially discharging accumulated old fat and oil. Furofuki, a daikon dish stewed for a long time, is highly recommended to reduce high cholesterol and treat obesity. It also helps to tone the intestines and is simply delicious!

2-inch square piece kombu, soaked with a little water

1 medium daikon, cut into 1-inch rounds (about 2 cups)

1 medium leek, sliced into 2-inch diagonals (about 2 cups)

SHIITAKE BROTH (page 98) or water

few pinches of sea salt

1 teaspoon mirin (optional)

1 teaspoon shoyu

scallions or parsley, for garnish

SWEET MISO SAUCE

2 tablespoons barley miso

2 tablespoons brown rice syrup

1 teaspoon lemon zest

1. In a heavy pot, place kombu on the bottom, layer daikon rounds above, and then add leek on top. Pour enough shiitake broth or water to just cover the daikon layer. Add a few pinches of sea salt on top.

2. Over a medium flame, bring to a boil, cover, and simmer for 25–30 minutes until daikon rounds become tender.

3. Add mirin, if using, and shoyu and continue to simmer for 5 minutes.

4. To make the sweet miso sauce, grind barley miso, brown rice syrup, and 1 tablespoon of water in a suribachi or mortar. Transfer into a small saucepan and simmer for a few minutes. Remove from flame and add lemon zest.

5. Serve furofuki daikon with sweet miso sauce and garnish.

EDAMAME ASPIC

SERVES 5-6

Edamame, a popular green soybean snack, may also be used in vegetable dishes, in soups, or made into sweets. In this dish, edamame beans are processed into a mousse-like aspic with a rich, savory flavor.

3⅓ cups KOMBU AND SHIITAKE BROTH (page 98), divided

2½ tablespoons agar-agar flakes

½ teaspoon sea salt

1½ cups shelled edamame, blanched and puréed in a food processor

1 tablespoon kuzu, dissolved in 2 tablespoons cold water

1 tablespoon shoyu

1 teaspoon brown rice vinegar

1 teaspoon umeboshi vinegar

1 additional tablespoon kuzu, dissolved in 2 tablespoons cold water

grated ginger and scallions, for garnish

1. In a saucepan, combine 2 cups of kombu and shiitake broth and agar-agar and bring to a boil. Over a medium-low flame, stir gently until agar-agar dissolves completely.

2. Add sea salt, edamame purée, and 1 tablespoon dissolved kuzu, and continue to simmer for about 5 minutes until everything is mixed well and the kuzu turns transparent.

3. Pour into a heat-safe glass container and let cool to room temperature or place in the refrigerator.

4. In a saucepan, bring remaining 1⅓ cups of broth to a boil and flavor with shoyu and vinegars.

5. Add remaining 1 tablespoon dissolved kuzu and stir well until the kuzu turns transparent and the sauce thickens.

6. Cut edamame aspic into nice squares on a plate, and serve with sauce and garnish.

VEGETABLE TEMPURA

SERVES 5

Vegetable tempura, battered and deep-fried, is crispy, tasty, and satisfying. Most people consider deep-frying to be an unhealthy way of cooking; however, it is beneficial to serve deep-fried food for the ricÚess it provides for children and adults who need more oil in their diet. As long as you are using a good-quality high-heat oil, for healthy people tempura is a great dish to serve once or twice a week.

VEGETABLE TEMPURA

1 cup pastry flour

broccoli, cut into 5 florets

carrot, sliced into 5 pieces

kabocha squash, sliced into 5 pieces

zucchini, sliced into 5 pieces

sweet potato, sliced into 5 pieces

5 string beans

¼ teaspoon sea salt

2 teaspoons kuzu

safflower oil, for deep-frying

DIPPING SAUCE

½ cup SHIITAKE BROTH (page 98) or water

1 tablespoon shoyu

1 teaspoon grated ginger

½–1 tablespoon mirin (optional)

lemon slices, for garnish

1. Place flour in a large mixing bowl. Coat each vegetable slice one by one with flour and place on a plate.
2. Make tempura batter by adding sea salt, kuzu, and 1 cup of chilled water to the mixing bowl with the remaining flour. Keep batter in refrigerator until the deep-frying oil is ready.
3. Place safflower oil in a heavy pot and heat over a medium-high flame until about 350°F. To check the temperature, place a wood chopstick in the oil. If you see fine bubbles actively coming out of the chopstick, it is ready to fry.
4. Quickly dip each vegetable slice into the batter. Fry in oil until crispy and the color turns light yellow.
5. Place deep-fried pieces on a kitchen towel to drain excess oil. You can fry a few pieces together in a pot, but do not put too many pieces in at once, which would lower the oil temperature.
6. To make the dipping sauce, heat shiitake broth or water, shoyu, grated ginger, and mirin, if using, in a small pan until boiling.
7. Serve tempura with dipping sauce and garnish.

CHEF'S TIP: *Grated ginger and grated daikon are very nice to serve with tempura. They help to digest deep-fried dishes. Mushrooms and onions also make nice tempura.*

Roasted Beet Salad with Orange-Mustard Dressing
(see recipe on page 188)

DELECTABLE SALADS AND FLAVORFUL DRESSINGS

"I try to be firm but gentle in slicing and proceed in a calm, orderly manner. Vegetables that are cut in a disorderly or chaotic fashion will transmit that energy to those who eat them. Food is alive and from field to dinner table should be treated with respect."
—AVELINE KUSHI

BEAN SPROUT SALAD (KOREAN NAMUL STYLE)

SERVES 4–5

This light, mildly crunchy salad will cool and relax you. The Korean-style seasoning is slightly pungent but rich and tasty.

pinch of sea salt

1 (5-ounce) package bean sprouts (5 cups)

2 teaspoons toasted sesame oil

2 teaspoons shoyu

2 teaspoons finely grated ginger

1 teaspoon apple cider vinegar, or to taste

1–2 tablespoons ground sesame seeds

finely chopped scallions, for garnish

1. Bring 8 cups of water to a boil in a large pot. Add a pinch of sea salt.
2. Blanch bean sprouts. Drain well in a strainer.
3. Place blanched bean sprouts in a large bowl while they are still hot and season with toasted sesame oil, shoyu, ginger, and apple cider vinegar.
4. Gently mix well and toss with ground sesame seeds. Top with garnish.

CAESAR SALAD WITH SOURDOUGH CROUTONS

SERVES 4–5

This vegan Caesar salad is very satisfying even for non-vegans. Homemade sourdough croutons provide a satisfying, crunchy texture!

CAESAR DRESSING

6 ounces silken tofu

1 tablespoon lemon juice

½–1 clove garlic

1 tablespoon white miso

½ teaspoon umeboshi vinegar

½–1 tablespoon olive oil

sea salt, to taste

black pepper, to taste

SOURDOUGH BREAD CROUTONS

5 cups 1-inch sourdough bread cubes

2 tablespoons olive oil

1 tablespoon maple syrup (optional, for sweet flavor)

⅛ teaspoon sea salt

black pepper, to taste

1 head romaine lettuce, washed, spun in a salad spinner, and torn into bite-size pieces

TO MAKE THE DRESSING:

1. Place tofu and lemon juice in a food processor. Process for 1 minute.
2. Add remaining ingredients and process for a few minutes until mixed well. Taste, adjusting flavor if necessary.

TO MAKE THE CROUTONS:

1. Preheat oven to 350°F.
2. Place bread cubes in a large mixing bowl.
3. Add remaining ingredients to the bowl. Toss and mix well with the bread cubes.
4. Line a baking pan with parchment paper and arrange bread cubes evenly.
5. Bake for 10–15 minutes until golden and crispy.
6. Remove from oven and let cool to room temperature.

TO ASSEMBLE THE SALAD:

1. Place lettuce in a salad bowl and toss with the dressing.
2. Top salad with sourdough croutons and serve immediately.

CHEF'S TIP: *You can make the croutons (yields 4 cups) and the dressing (yields 1 cup) ahead of time. The croutons will keep in an airtight jar at room temperature for a few days. The Caesar dressing will keep in the refrigerator for 3–4 days.*

ROASTED BEET SALAD WITH ORANGE-MUSTARD DRESSING

SERVES 7–8

On a warm sunny day, if Sachi finds seasonal beets at the local farmers' market, it's time to make this salad. The natural sweet flavor from the roasted beets and the crispness of the fresh lettuce combine to make a real treat. This is also great to serve at a party or bring to a potluck.

3 medium-size beets

2 tablespoons extra-virgin olive oil

1 tablespoon umeboshi vinegar

1 tablespoon apple cider vinegar

2–3 fresh heads of lettuce (such as romaine, butter, or mesclun)

ORANGE-MUSTARD DRESSING

½ cup orange juice

¼ cup extra-virgin olive oil

2 tablespoons Dijon mustard

dash of shoyu

sea salt, to taste

black pepper, to taste

TO ROAST THE BEETS:

1. Preheat oven to 400°F. Wrap each beet with parchment paper and then wrap again with aluminum foil. Place wrapped beets on baking tray.

2. Roast in the oven for about 45 minutes to 1 hour until beets become tender. Check beets with a skewer by poking beet after 45 minutes. Set aside to cool.

3. In a large bowl, combine olive oil and vinegars to make a marinade. Once beets cool down, peel skin off by hand and slice into half-moons. Place sliced beets into the marinade and let sit for 30 minutes.

TO ASSEMBLE THE SALAD:

1. Wash each leaf of the lettuce and spin to remove excess water. Tear into big bite sizes and put into a salad bowl.

2. In a jar, mix dressing ingredients.

3. Place lettuce in a serving bowl and top with marinated beets.

4. Drizzle dressing over the bowl, toss, and serve immediately.

SWEET POTATO SALAD

SERVES **4–5**

This is very similar to ordinary potato salad, but it is much healthier and the Japanese sweet potato and the tangy creamy dressing combine for a rich and flavorful medley.

SWEET POTATO SALAD

1 medium Japanese sweet potato, diced (2 cups)

few pinches of sea salt

1 cup chopped broccoli or broccolini (bite-size florets)

1 cup chopped cauliflower (bite-size florets)

½ cup sliced red onion (thin half-moons), marinated with ½ teaspoon umeboshi vinegar

black pepper (optional)

parsley, for garnish

DRESSING

4–5 tablespoons TOFU SOUR CREAM (page 227) or TOFU MAYONNAISE (page 226)

1 tablespoon Dijon mustard

½–1 teaspoon umeboshi vinegar

1. Soak diced sweet potato with water in a mixing bowl for 5 minutes. Drain well.
2. In a steamer, steam sweet potato with a few pinches of sea salt until soft. Set aside to cool.
3. Repeat the same process with broccoli and cauliflower. Set individual vegetables aside to cool.
4. Mix dressing ingredients in a small bowl. Place all the vegetables and marinated red onion in a mixing bowl. Add the dressing and black pepper, if desired. Mix gently.
5. Taste, adjusting flavor if necessary. Serve with garnish.

 VARIATION | Other types of sweet potato or winter squash can be substituted for Japanese sweet potato.

TAHINI DRESSING

MAKES ⅔ CUP

This sauce makes a delicious dressing for salads, dips, and other special dishes such as falafel.

3 tablespoons tahini

2 tablespoons lemon juice

1 teaspoon umeboshi vinegar

2 teaspoons white miso

dash of shoyu or tamari

1. Place all ingredients and ¼ cup of water in a blender and blend until smooth.
2. Add more water if necessary to reach desired consistency.
3. Taste, adjusting flavor with shoyu or tamari if necessary.
4. Store leftover dressing in a jar and keep in the refrigerator for 4–5 days.

VARIATION | See LEMON-TAHINI DRESSING (page 206).

PUMPKIN SEED DRESSING

MAKES 1½ CUPS

Served over blanched vegetables, steamed greens, or pressed salad, this creamy, healthy dressing can be enjoyed several times a week.

½ cup raw pumpkin seeds

2–3 teaspoons umeboshi paste

½ cup finely chopped parsley

2 tablespoons lemon juice

1. Wash seeds and roast in a skillet. When roasted, the seeds should be slightly brown, puffy, and break easily between your fingers. Let cool to room temperature.
2. Place roasted seeds in a food processor and blend until finely ground.
3. Add the rest of the ingredients and ¾–1 cup of water and blend until smooth. Adjust consistency and flavor to taste.
4. Store leftover dressing in a jar and keep in the refrigerator for 3–4 days.

LEMON–POPPY SEED VINAIGRETTE

MAKES 1¼ CUPS

This vinaigrette is perfect for a summer day salad.

¼ cup lemon juice

1 tablespoon lemon zest

1 teaspoon Dijon mustard

2 tablespoons rice syrup

¼ cup chopped onion

2 teaspoons shoyu

5 tablespoons olive oil

sea salt, to taste

3 tablespoons poppy seeds, lightly toasted

1. Place all the ingredients except poppy seeds in a blender. Blend until the texture is smooth.
2. Place the mixture in a mixing bowl. Add poppy seeds and mix well with a whisk. Adjust consistency and flavor if necessary.
3. Store leftover vinaigrette in a jar and keep in the refrigerator for 3–4 days.

LEMON-SHALLOT VINAIGRETTE

MAKES ½ CUP

This vinaigrette is easy to make and yields a delightful lemony flavor.

1 medium shallot, minced (3 tablespoons)

3 tablespoons lemon juice

3 teaspoons umeboshi vinegar

1 teaspoon Dijon mustard

2 tablespoons olive oil

black pepper (optional)

1. In a mixing bowl, mix all the ingredients well.
2. Adjust consistency and flavor if necessary. Set aside to settle flavors for 10 minutes.
3. Store leftover vinaigrette in a jar and keep in the refrigerator for 2–3 days.

SCALLION-UME DRESSING

MAKES ¾ CUP

This light, refreshing dressing is especially tasty served over blanched or steamed vegetables.

3 scallions, finely chopped (½ cup)

2 teaspoons umeboshi vinegar

2 teaspoons sesame oil

2 teaspoons brown rice vinegar

1. Place all the ingredients and ½ cup of water in a blender and blend until smooth.
2. Adjust consistency and flavor if necessary.
3. Store leftover dressing in a jar and keep in the refrigerator for 2–3 days.

SUNFLOWER SEED WITH ARUGULA DRESSING

MAKES 1¾ CUPS

The pungent, peppery flavor of the arugula blends nicely with the nutty creaminess of the sunflower seeds in this delightful dressing.

½ cup raw sunflower seeds

1 cup coarsely chopped arugula

1 tablespoon umeboshi vinegar

1 tablespoon brown rice vinegar

1 teaspoon brown rice syrup

1 teaspoon white miso

1 tablespoon olive oil

sea salt, to taste

1. Rinse and drain sunflower seeds. Lightly roast in a skillet on medium-low flame for 10 minutes until seeds become shiny and a light golden color. Stir constantly to prevent burning.
2. Place all the ingredients and 1 cup of water in a blender and blend until smooth. Adjust the consistency and flavor if necessary. Dressing should not be runny, nor should it be as thick as a dip.
3. Store leftover dressing in a jar and keep in the refrigerator for 2–3 days.

VARIATION | Instead of arugula, use watercress or parsley.

ORANGE-BALSAMIC VINAIGRETTE

MAKES 1 CUP

This is a great vinaigrette for fresh salad.

½ cup orange juice

1½ tablespoons umeboshi
vinegar

2 tablespoons balsamic
vinegar

2 teaspoons shoyu or
tamari

2 teaspoons Dijon mustard

4 tablespoons olive oil

sea salt, to taste

dash of black pepper
(optional)

1. In a mixing bowl, mix all the ingredients well.
2. Taste, adjusting consistency and flavor by adding sea salt if necessary.
3. Store leftover dressing in a jar and keep in the refrigerator for 2–3 days.

TANGERINE-UME DRESSING

MAKES ⅔ CUP

This tangy dressing is delightful served over pressed salads and blanched or steamed vegetables.

½ cup tangerine juice

1½ tablespoons umeboshi
vinegar

1 tablespoon olive oil

dash of shoyu or tamari
(optional)

1. In a mixing bowl, mix all the ingredients well.
2. Adjust consistency and flavor if necessary.
3. Store leftover dressing in a jar and keep in the refrigerator for 2–3 days.

Umeboshi Vinegar Pickles
(see recipe on page 199)

Shoyu / Tamari Pickles
(see recipe on page 199)

TASTY HOMEMADE
PICKLES

*"a butterfly also comes
to sip the vinegar from mums
and pickles"*

—BASHO

FERMENTATION IS AN AGE-OLD PROCESS OF FOOD PROCESSING. IT HAS BEEN USED to produce beer, wine, and sake; leaven bread and baked goods; make miso, shoyu, tempeh, and other soy products; culture cheese, yogurt, and other dairy products; cure olives; and make sauerkraut, kimchi, and other pickles. During the fermentation process, under anaerobic conditions, bacteria convert carbohydrates to organic compounds that enhance the qualities of the food or beverage being fermented.

Besides creating a diversity of flavors, tastes, aromas, and textures, fermentation helps preserve food and enrich its contents of protein, vitamins, minerals, and essential amino acids; improves digestion; eliminates antinutrients or harmful substances; and reduces cooking time and fuel use.

The major health benefit of fermentation is improved digestion. The enzymes, bacteria, and other microorganisms in fermented food strengthen the microbiome, which consists of trillions of bacteria in the small intestine and other regions of the body. This ecological community strengthens natural immunity, protects from pathogens, promotes assimilation, and improves blood and lymph production.

Pickles help digest grains and vegetables and have traditionally been eaten around the world. During fermentation, enzymes and bacteria change the sugar in pickled foods into

lactic acid. Lactic acid stimulates the appetite, strengthens the intestines, and improves assimilation of foodstuffs into the bloodstream. In macrobiotic cooking, a wide variety of pickles are made from root, round, and leafy green vegetables, as well as from some sea vegetables, fruit, and even flowers. Pickles may be made with shoyu, miso, umeboshi plum, bran, and other substances in addition to the more common salt.

UMEBOSHI VINEGAR PICKLES

MAKES 1 CUP *(see photo on page 196)*

These tangy, crunchy pickles are nice to serve with rice.

1 cup thinly sliced vegetables (such as radishes, carrots, and daikon)

2½ tablespoons umeboshi vinegar

1. Pack vegetables well in a jar.
2. Mix umeboshi vinegar with ½ cup of water and pour into the jar. Make sure the vegetables are fully submerged in the brine.
3. Cover with cheesecloth and use twine to hold it tight. Leave at room temperature for 1 day and then store in the refrigerator. After 1 day, it will be ready to eat. These pickles will keep in a refrigerator for up to 10 days.

VARIATION | This recipe is also great with fresh lotus root. If using lotus root, blanch them prior to pickling.

SHOYU / TAMARI PICKLES

MAKES 1½ CUPS *(see photo on page 196)*

These tangy shoyu pickles are a delicious accompaniment to your meal. Tamari may be used instead of shoyu for those sensitive to gluten.

2½–3 tablespoons shoyu or tamari

⅛ cup apple cider vinegar or brown rice vinegar

1½ cups sliced vegetables (such as onion, daikon, cauliflower, broccoli florets and its stem, etc.)

1. In a small bowl, combine shoyu or tamari with vinegar and ½ cup of water.
2. Pack vegetables in a glass jar and add liquid mixture. Make sure the vegetables are fully submerged in the brine.
3. Cover with cheesecloth and use twine to hold it tight. Leave at room temperature for 1 day and then store in the refrigerator. After 1 day, they will be ready to eat. These pickles will keep for up to 10 days.

HOMEMADE SAUERKRAUT

MAKES ABOUT 3 QUARTS

There's nothing as tasty as homemade sauerkraut, and it is actually quite simple to make! This cultured food strengthens digestion with its enzymes, while its flavor adds to the overall enjoyment of meals. There are endless ways to prepare sauerkraut. Here are three.

1 big head cabbage (about 3½ pounds)

1½–2 tablespoons sea salt

2 teaspoons caraway seeds

2 teaspoons juniper berries

1. Discard outer leaves of cabbage and save for later. Rinse cabbage head under cold running water and drain.

2. Cut head in quarters and remove cores. Shred cabbage and put in a large mixing bowl.

3. Toss with sea salt and other ingredients. Massage using your hands until the cabbage starts to release water. Massaging the cabbage with sea salt will break through the cell walls, and the cabbage will start to shine.

4. Sanitize a plate and place it on top of the cabbage and then put a weight on top of the plate. Leave for 30 minutes, allowing the water level to rise above the cabbage.

5. Transfer cabbage and liquid into a sanitized suitable vessel, such as a crock or glass jar. Pack cabbage firmly until it is completely submerged under the liquid. Use the thick outer leaves of the cabbage to cover the top of the shredded cabbage.

6. Arrange cabbage so it rests at least 4–5 inches below the top rim of the storage vessel and then cover the cabbage with a plate that fits inside the vessel.

7. Place a sanitized object, like a rock or a smaller jar, as a weight on the plate. This weight will force water out of the cabbage while keeping the cabbage submerged under the brine.

8. Cover the entire vessel with up to 3 layers of cheesecloth. Hold the cheesecloth in place with twine. Store at 70°F–75°F while fermenting. At this temperature, kraut will be fully fermented in about 2–3 weeks; at 60°F–65°F, fermentation may take 4–5 weeks.

9. Check the container several times a week and promptly remove surface scum or mold. When the lactic acid fermentation is taking place, there is a nice sour aroma and flavor. The fully fermented kraut may be kept tightly covered in the refrigerator for several months.

VARIATIONS | To make beautiful red sauerkraut, use the same amount of cabbage with the following ingredients: 2 tablespoons sea salt, 1–2 teaspoons grated ginger, 1 red beet (shredded), and 2 apples (thinly sliced). To make yellow, Indian-style flavored sauerkraut, use the same amount of cabbage with the following ingredients: 2 tablespoons sea salt, 2 tablespoons peeled and grated fresh turmeric root, 2 teaspoons cumin seeds, and 2 garlic cloves (grated). Follow the instructions above.

Wakame Salad with Amaranth and Pine Nuts
(see recipe on page 210)

APPETIZING
SEA VEGETABLES

"Let the sky rain potatoes;
let it thunder to the tune of Green-sleeves,
hail kissing-comfits and snow eryngoes [sea holly, an edible
English seaweed],
let there come a tempest of provocation . . ."
—SHAKESPEARE, MERRY WIVES OF WINDSOR

SEA VEGETABLES HAVE TRADITIONALLY BEEN EATEN BY MOST CULTURES AND SOCI-
eties. In the British Isles, sea holly, dulse, and Irish moss were popular. In modern times they
have been consumed primarily in the Far East and Polynesia. However, with the popularity of
sushi, nori is now enjoyed in America, Europe, and around the world.

As a small but important part of the macrobiotic way of eating, sea vegetables provide
many benefits. They are proportionately higher in iron, calcium, and other minerals than any
other food group, including meat and dairy food. They have many healing properties, including detoxifying the body of radiation and heavy metals. They also have been used for centuries
to beautify the skin and grow full, luxuriant hair.

Plants from the ocean also have a very different energy and vibration than plants grown
on land. They give supple, flexible energy and are especially beneficial in preventing and
relieving disorders affecting the heart and other blood vessels. Finally, by incorporating a
small, regular amount of food from the sea, which covers three-quarters of the planet, we
develop a more comprehensive mind and spirit than just eating food from the land, which
occupies the remaining one-quarter.

The following chart broadly summarizes the preparation and cooking time for different
sea veggies. When preparing your meals, please refer to the actual recipes in this book as
instructions for any given dish may vary slightly from this chart.

COOKING SEA VEGETABLES

TYPE	CLEANING	COOKING TIME	COOKED APPEARANCE	MAIN USES
AGAR-AGAR	none	4–10 minutes	translucent white	kanten (fruit puddings, mousses); vegetable aspic
ARAME	rinse 1–3 times	20–30 minutes	dark brown	side dish with sautéed root veggies; beans or tofu; in salads
DULSE	rinse	toasted 5–10 minutes	red/purple	dry roasted as a garnish for soups and salads
HIJIKI	rinse 1–3 times or soak 10 minutes	30–45 minutes	black	side dish with sautéed root vegetables; baked or boiled; in salads
KOMBU	rinse and soak 3–5 minutes	35–40 minutes	green/black	dashi broth; side dish; condiment; cooked with grains and beans
NORI	none	if not already toasted, toast 1 minute or less	green/black	sushi; rice balls; garnish for soups, salads, or noodles; casseroles; condiment
WAKAME	rinse and soak 5–10 minutes unless flakes	5–10 minutes	translucent green	miso soup; side dish; in salads

ARAME NOODLE SALAD

SERVES 3–4

This tasty sea vegetable and noodle salad is inspired by a recipe of Warren Kramer, renowned macrobiotic counselor from Boston. The arame harmonizes with the noodles, fresh greens, corn, and the creamy, tangy dressing. This salad is very relaxing yet nourishing, especially in the summertime.

ARAME NOODLE SALAD

½ cup arame, rinsed and soaked for 5 minutes

shoyu, to taste

6 ounces udon or somen noodles

1 cup fresh or frozen corn kernels

1 medium cucumber, sliced into matchsticks (1½ cups)

scallions, for garnish

LEMON-TAHINI DRESSING

4 tablespoons tahini

2 tablespoons lemon juice

1 tablespoon brown rice vinegar

1 tablespoon shoyu

½ tablespoon brown rice syrup

1 teaspoon umeboshi vinegar

TO MAKE THE ARAME NOODLE SALAD:

1. Quickly rinse and drain arame. Place in a saucepan and bring to a boil with 2 cups of water.
2. Cook over a low flame for about 15 minutes until tender. Season with a little shoyu and drain.
3. Cook noodles in boiling water according to the directions on the package.
4. Drain and rinse noodles under cool water.
5. Blanch corn. Mix with arame, noodles, and cucumber.
6. Serve with the dressing and garnish.

TO MAKE THE DRESSING:

1. Combine all ingredients in a suribachi or a blender.
2. Blend until smooth, slowly adding ⅓ cup of water to achieve a creamy consistency. Taste, adjusting consistency and flavor if necessary.

VARIATION | Use other types of noodles such as brown rice noodles, soba noodles, or quinoa noodles.

CUCUMBER-WAKAME SALAD WITH TANGERINES

SERVES 4–5

This recipe is a traditional Japanese sunomono salad, meaning "marinated with vinegar." The tangy wakame and crispy cucumber are surprisingly well matched with tangerines.

5-inch strip of dried wakame

3 cups sliced cucumber (thin rounds)

¼ teaspoon sea salt

1 teaspoon shoyu

1 tablespoon brown rice vinegar

¼ teaspoon umeboshi vinegar

1 teaspoon toasted sesame oil

½ cup peeled tangerine segments

ground toasted tan sesame seeds, for topping

1. Soak wakame with 1 cup water for 10 minutes, squeeze out water, and slice into bite-size pieces.
2. Place sliced cucumber in a mixing bowl. Sprinkle in sea salt, massage gently, and marinate for 15 minutes or until water is released from the cucumber.
3. While cucumber is marinating, make dressing by adding shoyu, vinegars, and sesame oil to a jar. Shake well to mix.
4. Squeeze cucumber to drain water. Place cucumber in a mixing bowl and add wakame and tangerine segments.
5. Toss with the dressing. Mix gently until all the ingredients harmonize well. Taste, adjusting flavor if necessary.
6. Serve with sesame seeds.

WAKAME SALAD WITH AMARANTH AND PINE NUTS

SERVES **4–5** *(see photo on page 202)*

In this innovative fusion dish, the tanginess of lemon and the ricÚess of roasted pine nuts and amaranth combine with the traditional flavor of Japanese wakame salad.

2 cups sliced cucumber (thin rounds)

pinch of sea salt

½ cup amaranth

2 tablespoons shoyu or 1½–2 tablespoons tamari

2 tablespoons lemon juice

5-inch strip dried wakame, soaked with 1 cup of water, drained, and sliced into bite-size pieces

¼ cup toasted pine nuts

1 tablespoon lemon zest

¼ cup finely sliced scallions, plus more for garnish

1. Place sliced cucumber in a mixing bowl. Sprinkle in sea salt, massage gently, and marinate for 15 minutes or until water is released from the cucumber.

2. While cucumber is marinating, bring ¾ cup of water to a boil in a saucepan, and add amaranth and a pinch of sea salt.

3. Bring to a boil again. Cover, place a flame deflector underneath the pot, and reduce flame to low. Simmer for 20 minutes.

4. Remove from flame and steam for 10 minutes.

5. Combine shoyu or tamari with lemon juice. Pour into amaranth, stir, and let cool to room temperature.

6. In a mixing bowl, add cucumber, wakame, pine nuts, lemon zest, and ¼ cup scallions. Add enough of the amaranth to coat all salad ingredients and serve with more scallions for garnish.

SIMPLE HIJIKI STEW

SERVES 4

Hijiki is a flavorful sea vegetable popular in Asian cooking and the contemporary macrobiotic community. Its long strands cook up thicker and darker than arame. It is especially tasty as a small side dish cooked with other vegetables or on top of a green salad.

2 tablespoons dried hijiki

1 tablespoon sesame oil

½ cup sliced onion (half-moons)

pinch of sea salt

½ cup sliced carrots (matchsticks)

shoyu, to taste

1. Soak hijiki with ½ cup of water for 15 minutes and drain.
2. In a stew pot, heat sesame oil and sauté onion with a pinch of sea salt for 3–4 minutes until translucent.
3. Layer hijiki and carrots on top of the onion and add enough water to cover the onion layer.
4. Bring to a boil, cover, reduce flame to medium-low, and simmer for 25–30 minutes.
5. Flavor with shoyu to taste, cover, and simmer for 5 minutes. Then cook uncovered until almost all the liquid evaporates.

"Our judgment naturally becomes clearer when we begin to take the foods of our ancestors, namely the whole grain cereals that are the cornerstone of all cultural development. With cereals we also can experience these past mentalities and we can realize the depth of ancient spiritual experience."

—MICHIO KUSHI

HIJIKI STEW WITH FRIED TOFU

SERVES 4–5

This recipe is inspired by Aveline Kushi's recipe. Hijiki is the king of seaweed, one of the top sources of all foods of iron, calcium, magnesium, and other minerals that help strengthen the blood and increase bone density. The deep-fried tofu makes this dish rich and satisfying.

1 cup sliced tofu (1 × 2-inch rectangular blocks)

safflower oil, for deep-frying

¼ cup dried hijiki, rinsed, soaked with 1 cup of water for 15 minutes, then drained

¼ cup sliced onion (half-moons)

⅓ cup sliced carrots (matchsticks)

1–1½ tablespoons shoyu or tamari, or to taste

scallions, for garnish

1. Press tofu blocks for 15 minutes and pat dry.
2. Heat safflower oil to 350°F. Deep fry tofu blocks in hot oil until golden brown. Fry only a couple of blocks at a time to maintain oil temperature. Put them on paper towels to drain off any excess oil.
3. Wash the hijiki and place in a saucepan. Add onion and carrots and then put the fried tofu on top.
4. Add just enough water to cover the hijiki but not the vegetables and tofu. Add shoyu or tamari and bring to a boil.
5. Cover, reduce flame to low, and simmer for about 30 minutes. Add a little more shoyu or tamari to create a mildly salty taste and continue to simmer until almost all the remaining liquid has evaporated.
6. Mix gently and serve with garnish.

VARIATION | Adding corn kernels at the end of cooking gives this dish extra sweetness and a bright color.

HIJIKI WITH ALMOND SAUCE

SERVES **4–5**

The creaminess of the almond sauce makes for a rich and savory experience that can be enjoyed by all, even those who are new to seaweed.

1 tablespoon sesame oil

1 medium onion, sliced into thin half-moons (2 cups)

few pinches of sea salt

¼ cup dried hijiki, rinsed and soaked with 1 cup of water for 15 minutes, then drained

1 cup sliced carrots (matchsticks)

1–1½ tablespoons shoyu

1–1½ tablespoons almond butter

½ cup fresh or frozen corn

scallions or parsley, for garnish

1. Heat sesame oil in a saucepan and sauté onion with a few pinches of sea salt for 3–4 minutes until translucent.
2. Layer hijiki and carrots on top of the onion and add ½ cup of water to cover just the onion layer.
3. Bring to a boil, reduce flame to medium-low, cover, and simmer for 20 minutes.
4. In a small bowl, mix shoyu and almond butter with 1–2 tablespoons of water.
5. Add shoyu and almond butter mixture to the saucepan and simmer for about 5 minutes until the sauce becomes creamy and smooth. If the sauce is too thick, add more water.
6. Add corn on top and simmer for another 5 minutes.
7. Taste, adjusting flavor if necessary, and serve with garnish.

SEAWEED-NUT CRUNCH

MAKES **4** CUPS

This snack is a great way to consume seaweed. A savory delight filled with minerals, it is great for busy bees and as a nutritious snack for kids. It can also be served as a topping on morning porridge.

4 tablespoons sesame oil

¼ cup brown rice syrup

1½ cups whole or coarsely chopped almonds

⅓ cup sesame seeds

1 tablespoon aonori flakes

6 sheets sushi nori, torn into bite-size pieces

1 tablespoon shoyu

1. Preheat oven to 200°F.

2. In a skillet, heat sesame oil and rice syrup over medium flame and cook until the liquid bubbles.

3. Add almonds, sesame seeds, aonori, and sushi nori, and sauté for about 10 minutes over a medium-low flame.

4. Season with shoyu and continue to stir for a few more minutes over a low flame.

5. Place the seaweed-nut mixture on a baking sheet lined with parchment paper. Oven roast the mixture for 30–40 minutes, mixing occasionally. Bake until almonds become shiny and golden in color.

6. Remove from the oven and let cool to room temperature. When it cools down, the texture becomes crunchy and it is ready to serve!

VARIATIONS | It is also nice to use walnuts and pecans instead of almonds. Aonori is green seaweed flakes from Japan. You can substitute nori or dulse for aonori. For a gluten-free option, substitute tamari for shoyu.

Carrot Marinara Sauce
(see recipe on page 225)

CONDIMENTS, SAUCES, SPREADS, AND DIPS

"Eat bread and salt and speak the truth."
—RUSSIAN PROVERB

SCALLION-MISO CONDIMENT

This savory condiment blends sharp, sour, and mildly sweet tastes and is an excellent accompaniment to whole grains, beans, vegetables, and other dishes.

1 bunch scallions with roots

1–1½ tablespoons miso
(barley miso, brown rice
miso, or chickpea miso)

1 tablespoon sesame oil

1. Wash scallions very well, including the roots. Slice scallions very finely and place the roots and the white and green parts into three separate bowls.

2. Place miso and 2 tablespoons of water in a small suribachi or a mortar and purée into paste.

3. Heat sesame oil in a stainless steel skillet. Sauté roots of the scallions, then add the white parts, and finally the green parts for a few minutes until the color turns vibrant.

4. Make a little hollow in the center of the scallions and place the miso paste in the center of the skillet. Cover and simmer for a few minutes.

5. Mix well and serve. Store leftover condiment in a glass jar and keep in the refrigerator for 2–3 days.

VARIATIONS | You may substitute 5 tablespoons of roasted and mashed sesame seeds for the oil. A touch of brown rice vinegar, mirin, or rice syrup may also be added.

SUNFLOWER WAKAME CONDIMENT

MAKES 1 TABLESPOON

Sunflower seeds give this condiment a rich, soothing texture and flavor. This condiment goes well on top of grains.

3–4 inch strip dried wakame

8 tablespoons sunflower seeds

1. Cut wakame strip into small pieces. Carefully dry roast in a cast-iron skillet over a low flame until wakame becomes crisp but not burnt.
2. In a suribachi, grind wakame into a fine powder. Transfer wakame powder to a bowl and set aside.
3. Rinse sunflower seeds and then lightly roast in the same skillet until golden.
4. Add the roasted sunflower seeds to the same suribachi and coarsely grind.
5. Add the wakame powder back into the suribachi and grind together with sunflower seeds.
6. Store leftover condiment in a glass jar for up to 1 week.

NORI CONDIMENT

MAKES 1 CUP

This tasty sea vegetable condiment nourishes the bones and the lymph and reproductive systems. Serve on top of grains or porridge.

5 sheets sushi nori, torn by hand into small pieces

1–2 teaspoons shoyu

½–1 teaspoon ginger juice (optional)

1. Place sushi nori and ¾ cup of water in a small saucepan. Mix well.
2. Bring to a gentle boil over a medium flame.
3. Cover, reduce flame to low, and simmer for about 15 minutes until the nori dissolves well. Stir occasionally.
4. Add shoyu and ginger juice, if using, and simmer for 5 minutes.
5. Store leftover condiment in a bowl or glass jar and keep in the refrigerator for 3–4 days.

GOMASHIO

MAKES 1 CUP (18:1 RATIO)

This roasted sesame seed and sea salt sprinkle is the most commonly used condiment in the macrobiotic community, bringing fresÚess and flavor to many recipes. It adds a delicious accent to your grain dishes. A sprinkle of gomashio on a serving of rice helps alkalize the blood and relieve tiredness. Because of the salt base, a moderate mixture of seeds and salt is recommended. The ratio 18:1 is considered to be the average. Store-bought gomashio is usually much saltier—another reason to make your own gomashio at home.

2 teaspoons sea salt

¾ cup tan or black sesame seeds

1. Dry roast sea salt in a stainless-steel frying pan over a medium-low flame until some moisture evaporates and the color turns slightly gray.

2. Place sea salt into a suribachi and grind with a surikogi into a fine powder.

3. Wash sesame seeds in a fine mesh strainer and drain well. Add to the same skillet and roast over a medium flame with constant stirring to prevent burning. To test whether the seeds are done, use a metal spoon to scoop up the seeds. They are done when they no longer stick to the spoon.

4. Add seeds to the ground sea salt in the suribachi. Slowly grind seeds in an even, circular motion with the surikogi. Grind until 80 percent of the seeds are crushed. Mix well to make sure the sea salt is uniformly distributed through the sesame seeds. Allow the gomashio to cool and store in an airtight container like a glass jar.

CHEF'S TIP: *The gomashio will keep fresh for at least 2 weeks. Use sparingly over rice or other grains (generally no more than 1 teaspoon a day). Black sesame seeds are less fatty and roast faster than tan sesame seeds.*

SWEET VEGETABLE JAM

MAKES 2 CUPS

This makes a great condiment or spread for breakfast or a snack any time of day. The natural sweetness of the veggies relaxes the pancreas, stomach, and spleen, and the jam is a perfect macrobiotic spread or dip for people who crave simple sugar.

½ cup diced onion

1 cup chopped winter squash or sweet potato (bite-size pieces)

½ cup roll-cut carrots

pinch of sea salt

1. Place onion, winter squash or sweet potato, carrots, and ¼ cup of water in a small saucepan. Sprinkle a pinch of sea salt on top.

2. Bring to a boil over a medium flame, reduce flame to medium-low, cover, and simmer for 30–40 minutes until vegetables become very soft. If the water in the pan evaporates, add a little more water.

3. Place vegetables in a suribachi. Using a surikogi, mash everything into a creamy texture.

4. Store leftover jam in a glass jar and keep in the refrigerator for 2–3 days.

VARIATION | You can substitute 1–2 types of other sweet vegetables, such as yams, for those called for in this recipe; just use equal portions.

CARROT MARINARA SAUCE

MAKES **2** CUPS *(see photo on page 218)*

When served this sauce, people are amazed by how it tastes just like tomato marinara sauce. We also call it "No-mato Sauce." This scrumptious sauce is enjoyed by all and particularly appreciated by individuals avoiding nightshades. It goes well atop polenta or with pasta, lasagna, and other casserole dishes.

1 tablespoon olive oil

1 medium onion, diced (1 cup)

1 clove garlic, minced (optional)

3 medium carrots, diced (2 cups)

2 celery stalks, diced (1 cup)

¼ cup diced beet (optional, for a bright red color)

¼ teaspoon sea salt, plus few pinches

1 tablespoon white miso

1 tablespoon umeboshi paste

1 teaspoon umeboshi vinegar

¼ teaspoon dried basil (optional)

1. In a heavy pot, heat oil and sauté onion and garlic with a few pinches of sea salt for 3–4 minutes until the onion becomes translucent.
2. Add carrots, celery, beet, and ¼ cup of water. Sprinkle ¼ teaspoon sea salt on top and bring to a boil.
3. Cover the pot and simmer for 30–40 minutes until vegetables become tender. Set aside to cool.
4. Once cooled, blend vegetables in a food processor until the texture becomes smooth.
5. Pour sauce back into pot, cover, bring to a boil, reduce flame to low, and simmer for 10 minutes. Season with miso, umeboshi paste, and umeboshi vinegar. Add dried basil, if using, and simmer for another 5 minutes.

BALSAMIC REDUCTION SAUCE

This sauce is a great topping for pasta and risotto or lightly drizzled atop a dessert.

1 cup balsamic vinegar

1 tablespoon maple syrup (optional)

1. Heat balsamic vinegar in a small saucepan and bring to a boil. Reduce flame to low and simmer until volume reduces to about half. Set aside to cool.
2. For a sweeter sauce, add the maple syrup at the end of simmering.

TOFU MAYONNAISE

MAKES 1½ CUPS

This versatile vegan mayonnaise can be added to many dishes, such as pasta salad, tempeh cutlets, and coleslaw.

1 (14-ounce) package firm tofu, cut into quarters

3 tablespoons brown rice vinegar

1 tablespoon lemon juice

1 clove garlic, minced (optional, see tip)

1 tablespoon mustard

2 teaspoons white miso

2 teaspoons umeboshi vinegar

1 teaspoon brown rice syrup

2 tablespoons olive oil

sea salt, to taste

1. In a saucepan, bring 3 cups of water to a boil and boil tofu for 10 minutes. Make sure tofu is fully submerged under the boiling water. Drain and let cool to room temperature in a strainer.

2. In a food processor, place tofu, brown rice vinegar, and lemon juice. Blend well until smooth.

3. Add the rest of the ingredients except the olive oil and sea salt and blend until smooth and creamy.

4. Taste and add sea salt if necessary. Slowly pour in olive oil while the food processor is spinning.

5. Store leftover mayonnaise in a glass jar and keep in the refrigerator for 2–3 days.

CHEF'S TIP: *Oven-roasting garlic or sautéing it in a skillet with a little olive oil will take out its sharpness and enhance the dressing's flavor.*

TOFU TARTAR SAUCE

MAKES 2 CUPS

This sauce is great to serve with deep-fried croquettes. It is tangy and delicious, and the dill pickles help with digesting the oil.

1½ cups TOFU MAYONNAISE (above)

¼ cup unsweetened soy milk

black pepper, to taste (optional)

⅓ cup diced dill pickles or fresh cucumber

1. Place tofu mayonnaise, soy milk, and black pepper, if using, in a food processor.

2. Blend until texture is smooth and creamy.

3. Transfer mixture to a mixing bowl.

4. Add diced dill pickles and gently mix well.

5. Store leftover sauce in a glass jar and keep in the refrigerator for 2–3 days.

TOFU SOUR CREAM

MAKES 2 CUPS

Tofu sour cream is great with REFRIED PINTO BEANS (page 130) and BLACK BEAN STEW (page 126).

1 (14-ounce) package tofu, cut into quarters

4 tablespoons lemon juice

1 clove garlic (optional), minced and roasted or sautéed

1 tablespoon mustard

2 tablespoons umeboshi vinegar

1 tablespoon brown rice syrup

1 tablespoon safflower oil

sea salt, to taste

1. In a saucepan, bring 3 cups of water to a boil and boil tofu for 10 minutes. Make sure tofu is fully submerged under the boiling water. Drain and let cool to room temperature in a strainer.

2. In a food processor, blend tofu and lemon juice well for a couple of minutes until smooth.

3. Add other ingredients, except safflower oil and sea salt, and purée well. Taste, adjusting flavor with sea salt if necessary.

4. Add safflower oil and blend well until creamy.

5. Store leftover sour cream in a glass jar and keep in the refrigerator for 2–3 days.

CILANTRO SAUCE

MAKES 2 CUPS

The refreshing herby flavor of cilantro meshes with the tanginess of lemon to make the perfect sauce to accompany croquettes, fritters, and roasted vegetables.

1–2 cloves garlic, sliced

4½ tablespoons olive oil, divided

2 bunches cilantro, washed and chopped (4 cups)

½ cup lemon juice

½ cup apple juice

1 teaspoon sea salt

1 tablespoon rice vinegar

1 tablespoon umeboshi vinegar

1 teaspoon shoyu

black pepper (optional)

1. In a small skillet, lightly sauté garlic in ½ tablespoon of olive oil until golden.

2. Place garlic with remaining ingredients in a blender and blend until smooth.

3. Taste, adjusting flavor if necessary.

4. Store leftover sauce in a jar and keep in the refrigerator for 3–4 days.

HUMMUS

MAKES 3 CUPS

Hummus, the tasty traditional spread from the Middle East, is one of the world's most popular snacks. Serve with raw vegetables, pita bread, or in a sandwich.

1 cup dried chickpeas, sorted, washed, and soaked with 3 cups water

1-inch square piece kombu

HUMMUS SPREAD

2–3 tablespoons lemon juice

2–3 teaspoons umeboshi paste

2 tablespoons olive oil, plus more for topping

2 teaspoons white miso

1½ tablespoons tahini

1 clove garlic, raw, minced or roasted (optional)

sumac or smoked paprika powder for topping (optional)

TO MAKE THE CHICKPEAS:

1. Discard soaking water and rinse chickpeas.
2. Place kombu and chickpeas in a pressure cooker. Add water to cover ½ inch above the chickpeas. Bring to a boil uncovered, skimming off white foam as it arises on the surface.
3. Close the pressure cooker lid, bring up to pressure, and simmer for 50 minutes. Allow pressure to come down and then open the pot. Drain chickpeas and let them cool to room temperature, reserving the cooking water.

TO MAKE THE SPREAD:

1. In a food processor, place chickpeas and the rest of the ingredients. Save some chickpeas for topping.
2. Blend until texture becomes smooth and creamy.
3. Add some chickpea cooking water if the mixture is too dry to blend.
4. Serve hummus topped with olive oil, chickpeas, and sumac or smoked paprika powder, if desired.
5. Store leftover hummus in a glass jar and keep in the refrigerator for 2–3 days.

TEMPEH "TUNA" SALAD

SERVES 5-6

This scrumptious mock tuna salad has the texture, look, and taste of the original. It is a favorite travel food and virtually guaranteed to be taken for the "real thing" by those unfamiliar with vegan cuisine.

1 (8-ounce) package of tempeh

1-inch square piece kombu

½ cup finely diced red onion, marinated with 1 teaspoon umeboshi vinegar

1 celery stalk, finely diced

2 teaspoons chopped capers or sauerkraut

½–⅔ cup TOFU MAYONNAISE (page 226)

chopped dill and parsley, for garnish

1. Dice tempeh and steam with kombu for 25–30 minutes.
2. In a large suribachi, mash steamed tempeh with a pestle.
3. Add onion, celery, capers or sauerkraut, and tofu mayonnaise. Mix well and serve with garnish.

lentil-walnut paté   *tempeh "tuna" salad*

LENTIL-WALNUT PATÉ

MAKES 2 CUPS

This healthy paté is made with lentils, walnuts, mushrooms, and onions, and it makes an excellent vegan hors d'oeuvre.

1 cup dried brown lentils, sorted and washed

1 tablespoon olive oil

1 medium onion, diced (2 cups)

1–2 cloves garlic, minced

few pinches of sea salt

6 button mushrooms, sliced (1 cup)

1 teaspoon dried basil

1 cup walnuts

2 teaspoons white miso

1 teaspoon umeboshi paste

1. In a saucepan, place lentils and enough water to cover 1 inch above the lentils. Bring to a boil over medium flame, skimming off the white foam as it arises on the surface. Cover, reduce flame to low, and simmer for 40–50 minutes until beans become soft. Drain and set aside to cool.

2. Heat olive oil in a skillet and sauté onion and garlic with a few pinches of sea salt until the onion becomes a golden color.

3. Add mushrooms and dried basil, sauté for 5 minutes, and set aside to cool.

4. In a separate skillet, dry roast walnuts until the aroma becomes nutty and the texture turns crispy. Set aside to cool.

5. Place cooked lentils, onion-mushroom mixture, roasted walnuts, white miso, and umeboshi paste in a food processor. Blend until smooth. Taste, adjusting flavor if necessary.

6. Store leftover paté in a glass jar and keep in the refrigerator for 2–3 days.

CHEF'S TIP: *Perfectly roasted walnuts have a light brown/golden color. Be sure to use a medium flame, not high, and stir constantly, since nuts are easily burnt.*

Tiramisu with Cashew-Amazake Cream
(see recipe on page 266)

HEALTHY DESSERTS

"Sweets to the sweet."
—MARLOWE AND SHAKESPEARE, *HAMLET*

PEAR COMPOTE

SERVES 3-4

This simple dessert is delicious and comforting. Compotes are mild, easy to make, and nourishing.

2 pears, peeled, cored, and sliced diagonally into quarters

1 cup apple juice

few pinches of sea salt

1 heaping teaspoon kuzu, dissolved in 1 tablespoon cold water

few pinches of cinnamon powder (optional)

1 tablespoon lemon zest

½ tablespoon lemon juice

1. In a saucepan, place all the ingredients except kuzu, lemon zest, and lemon juice.
2. Bring to a boil, cover, and simmer for 20 minutes.
3. Take out the pears and place in a serving dish.
4. Add dissolved kuzu to the pot and keep stirring until the sauce thickens and the texture turns creamy. Stir in lemon zest and lemon juice.
5. Pour the sauce over the pears and serve.

WATERMELON KANTEN

SERVES 5-6

When watermelons are in season, this kanten is a must-have! This is a delicious summer dessert that children and the whole family will enjoy.

5–6 cups chopped watermelon

1 cup apple juice

pinch of sea salt

3 tablespoons agar-agar flakes

CASHEW CREAM (page 268), for topping (optional)

fresh mint leaves, for topping

1. Chop watermelon and blend into a smooth texture in a blender. The blended watermelon should yield 3 cups.

2. Combine apple juice, a pinch of sea salt, and agar-agar flakes in a saucepan. Bring to a boil, reduce flame to low, and simmer for 4–5 minutes until agar-agar flakes are completely dissolved, stirring constantly.

3. Pour dissolved agar-agar mixture into the blender on top of the watermelon and blend everything together.

4. Pour mixture into individual serving bowls and chill in the refrigerator until set.

5. Top with cashew cream, if using, and fresh mint and serve chilled.

VARIATIONS | Cantaloupes, honeydews, and strawberries may also be used to make blended kanten instead of watermelon.

Kanten

Kanten is a relaxing, cooling pudding-type dessert. It is especially delightful in summer but is suitable year-round. It is made with fruit and fruit juice gelled with agar-agar, a sea vegetable that usually comes in flakes. High in fiber and complex carbohydrates, agar-agar has shown promise in medical studies for diabetes, obesity, and related conditions.

LEMON KANTEN

SERVES 5–6

Lemon kanten is refreshing year-round. Its mild sourness is especially beneficial for the liver and gallbladder, and it will lighten you up with a lemony breeze!

2 cups apple juice

4 tablespoons agar-agar flakes

pinch of sea salt

2 tablespoons maple syrup

⅓–½ cup rice syrup

½ teaspoon vanilla extract

⅓ cup fresh lemon juice

1 tablespoon lemon zest

1. Combine apple juice, agar-agar flakes, and 1 cup of water in a saucepan and bring to a boil.
2. Add a pinch of sea salt, reduce flame to low, and simmer for 4–5 minutes until agar-agar flakes are completely dissolved, stirring constantly.
3. Add maple syrup and rice syrup and stir until dissolved.
4. Add vanilla extract and simmer for another minute.
5. Remove from the stovetop and add lemon juice and zest. Mix gently.
6. Pour the mixture into individual serving bowls or a large glass container and let cool to set.
7. Chill in refrigerator if desired. Serve as is or blend the set kanten in a food processor until smooth.

BLUEBERRY KANTEN

SERVES 4-5

This springtime kanten is wonderful, especially when blueberries are in season. ALMOND CREAM (page 268) is a great addition as a topping for this tasty dessert.

2 cups apple juice

pinch of sea salt

2 tablespoons agar-agar flakes

1 cup fresh or frozen blueberries

1 teaspoon kuzu, dissolved in ¼ cup apple juice

½ teaspoon vanilla extract (optional)

1. In a saucepan, place apple juice, a pinch of sea salt, and agar-agar flakes. Bring to a boil and reduce flame to low. Simmer for 4–5 minutes until agar-agar flakes are completely dissolved, stirring constantly.

2. Add blueberries, bring back to a boil over medium-low flame, and simmer until soft.

3. Gently add dissolved kuzu, stirring constantly for about 3 minutes until the mixture turns clear.

4. Turn off flame and add vanilla extract, if using. Pour the mixture into individual serving bowls or a large glass container. Set aside to cool to set. If you would like to serve this dish chilled, refrigerate for a few hours before serving.

STRAWBERRY MOUSSE

SERVES 4–5

This fruit pudding makes a delightful dessert or snack in the summer or warmer times of the year.

2 cups apple juice, plus a little more for blending

pinch of sea salt

3 tablespoons agar-agar flakes

½ teaspoon vanilla extract

2 cups fresh strawberry halves, plus more for garnish

1. Place apple juice, sea salt, and agar-agar flakes in a saucepan. Bring to a boil, reduce flame to low, and simmer for 4–5 minutes until the agar-agar flakes are completely dissolved, stirring constantly.

2. Remove from flame and add vanilla extract.

3. Pour apple juice mixture into a heat-safe glass container and add 2 cups of fresh strawberries.

4. Let cool to room temperature. Refrigerate until it sets.

5. Blend kanten in food processor or blender, adding a little apple juice if needed.

6. Serve with more strawberries as garnish.

VARIATION | Add 1 tablespoon of tahini or almond butter to the blend for a rich, creamy taste. For a sweeter mousse, add 1 tablespoon of maple or rice syrup.

"Do you remember the Shire, Mr. Frodo? It'll be spring soon. And the orchards will be in blossom. And the birds will be nesting in the hazel thicket. And they'll be sowing the summer barley in the lower fields . . . and eating the first of the strawberries with cream. Do you remember the taste of strawberries?"
—J. R. R. TOLKIEN, *THE LORD OF THE RINGS*

RASPBERRY-AMAZAKE MOUSSE

SERVES 4–5

This dessert is an example of "less is more" and is simply amazing. The infused raspberry flavor melds nicely with the rich, creamy texture.

⅔ cup fresh or frozen raspberries

1½ tablespoons agar-agar flakes

1–1½ tablespoons brown rice syrup

2 cups blended amazake

2 pinches of sea salt

2 teaspoons kuzu, dissolved in ¼ cup cold water

1 teaspoon vanilla extract

AMAZAKE CREAM (page 269), for topping (optional)

1. In a food processor or blender, blend raspberries and strain out the seeds to make ⅓ cup puréed raspberries. Set aside.

2. In a saucepan over a medium flame, place agar-agar flakes and 1 cup of water. Bring to a boil, reduce flame to low, and simmer for 4–5 minutes until the flakes are completely dissolved, stirring constantly.

3. Add brown rice syrup, amazake, and sea salt. Slowly bring to a boil again while continuously stirring.

4. Reduce flame to low and add dissolved kuzu, vanilla extract, and puréed raspberries. Stir for 2–3 minutes until everything harmonizes together.

5. Place the mixture into a large glass container or individual serving bowls. Let cool to room temperature, and refrigerate until the mousse sets.

6. Serve with amazake cream, if using.

VARIATION | Blueberries or other types of berries can be substituted for raspberries.

CHEF'S TIP: *If using homemade amazake, you will find it contains grains of rice. To achieve a smooth texture, blend amazake until creamy. Add water if it's too thick. Strain out the rice bran after blending. Adjust amount of rice syrup used depending on the sweetness of the amazake.*

MATCHA GREEN TEA MOUSSE

SERVES 3–4

If you are a green tea or *matcha* fan, this mousse will put you on cloud nine. It is a decadent dessert for a special treat.

2 tablespoons agar-agar flakes

2 tablespoons matcha powder

2 tablespoons maple syrup

3 tablespoons brown rice syrup

1/16 teaspoon sea salt

2 cups soy milk or almond milk

AMAZAKE CREAM (page 269), for topping (optional)

1. Place agar-agar flakes and ½ cup of water in a saucepan. Bring to a boil over a medium flame, reduce flame to medium-low, and simmer for 4–5 minutes until agar-agar flakes are completely dissolved, stirring constantly.

2. In a small mixing bowl, sift the matcha powder using a tea strainer, and then dissolve in 2 tablespoons of hot water, mixing well with a whisk until smooth. Set aside.

3. Add maple syrup, brown rice syrup, and sea salt to the agar-agar mixture, and stir everything until it dissolves.

4. Pour in soy milk or almond milk slowly as you are stirring. Keep stirring over a medium-low flame while simmering for 5–10 minutes until mixture becomes hot but before it starts to boil. Do not boil soy milk or almond milk.

5. Keep the flame low. Add matcha mixture to saucepan, stirring constantly to blend and harmonize everything together.

6. Pour the mixture into a large heat-safe glass container or individual serving bowls. Let cool to room temperature and place in the refrigerator for a few hours to set.

7. Serve with amazake cream, if using.

MOCHA CUSTARD MOUSSE

SERVES 6–8

Made with grain coffee, almond butter, and natural sweeteners, this custard will delight and satisfy your family or friends at the end of the meal. Topping with orange slices, berries, or other fruit makes a perfect garnish.

1 cup apple juice

5 tablespoons agar-agar flakes

¼ teaspoon sea salt

1½ tablespoons almond butter

2 cups soy or other nondairy milk, divided

3 tablespoons grain coffee powder

⅓ cup rice syrup or ¼ cup maple syrup

1 teaspoon vanilla extract

¼ teaspoon cinnamon powder

1. In a large saucepan, combine apple juice, agar-agar flakes, sea salt, and ½ cup of water. Bring to a boil, reduce flame to low, and simmer for 4–5 minutes until the flakes are completely dissolved, stirring constantly.

2. In a small bowl, dissolve almond butter in ½ cup of soy milk. Add this mixture into the saucepan and continue stirring.

3. Add grain coffee powder and then slowly pour in the remaining 1½ cups of milk.

4. Add syrup and continue stirring until everything blends well.

5. Add vanilla and cinnamon. Simmer for 3 minutes.

6. Pour into a large heat-safe glass container or individual serving bowls. Let cool to room temperature. Refrigerate for 1 hour until it sets.

7. In a food processor or blender, blend mixture into a smooth texture. Pour into individual serving cups and serve.

APPLE MILLET CAKE

SERVES 8 (9-INCH PIE OR TART PAN OR 8 × 6-INCH GLASS CONTAINER)

This is a simple, mildly sweet dessert for everybody to enjoy. This unbaked cake is also suitable for people who are avoiding baked flour products and those who limit desserts for healing. It is a simple yet hearty cake.

MILLET CRUST

½ cup millet, washed and soaked with 1 cup water overnight, reserve soaking water

1 cup apple juice

2 tablespoons chopped walnuts

pinch of sea salt

APPLE KANTEN FILLING

1½ cups apple juice

2 tablespoons agar-agar flakes

2 pinches of sea salt

1 big apple (Gala, Pink Lady, or other crisp type), cored and thinly sliced

2 tablespoons apricot jam (no-added-sugar, fruit-sweetened jam)

1 heaping teaspoon kuzu, dissolved in 1 tablespoon cold water

dash of vanilla extract (optional)

1 tablespoon lemon zest

TO MAKE THE MILLET CRUST:

1. Place millet with its soaking water, apple juice, walnuts, and a pinch of sea salt in a pot.
2. Bring to a boil over a medium flame. Place a flame deflector underneath the pot, cover, and reduce the flame. Simmer for 25–30 minutes until millet becomes soft. Mix well occasionally.
3. Gently mix with a wooden spatula and pour into a large heat-safe glass container or a pie pan. Set aside to cool.

TO MAKE APPLE KANTEN FILLING:

1. Combine apple juice, agar-agar flakes, sea salt, and ½ cup of water in a saucepan. Bring to a boil, reduce flame to low, and simmer for 4–5 minutes until agar-agar flakes are completely dissolved, stirring constantly.
2. Blanch apple slices in the apple juice mixture until the apple skin turns a bright color. Set apple slices aside.
3. In a small bowl, mix apricot jam and dissolved kuzu. Add to the saucepan with the agar-agar mixture and gently stir until translucent.
4. Add vanilla extract, if using. Turn off flame, add lemon zest, and mix gently.
5. Place blanched apple slices on the millet crust, aligning them in rows.
6. Slowly pour kanten sauce over the sliced apples. Let cool to set. Chill in refrigerator if desired. Slice into 8 pieces and serve.

PEACH COUSCOUS CAKE

SERVES 8 (9-INCH PIE OR TART PAN)

Couscous makes a delicious, fluffy, mildly sweet cake. Couscous cake is a favorite at parties, holidays, and other special occasions.

COUSCOUS CAKE

1½ cups apple juice

pinch of sea salt

¾ cup whole wheat couscous

PEACH TOPPING

1½ cups apple juice

1½ tablespoons agar-agar flakes

pinch of sea salt

1 tablespoon lemon zest

3 cups sliced fresh peaches or 16 ounces frozen peaches, thawed

TO MAKE THE COUSCOUS CAKE:

1. In a saucepan, combine apple juice and sea salt. Bring to a boil over medium flame. Pour couscous into the saucepan, stir, and cover the pan. Remove from flame and let sit for 10–15 minutes.
2. Open the lid and stir couscous gently with a wooden spoon. Place couscous in a 9-inch pie or tart pan and press down evenly to half the height of the pan. Cover and let cool while you prepare the topping.

TO MAKE THE PEACH TOPPING:

1. In a saucepan, combine apple juice, agar-agar flakes, and sea salt. Bring to a boil, reduce flame to low, and simmer for 4–5 minutes until agar-agar flakes are completely dissolved, stirring constantly. Remove from flame and add lemon zest.
2. Place peaches on couscous cake, aligning them in rows. Pour liquid gently and evenly over peaches and couscous.
3. Let cool to set. Chill in refrigerator if desired. Slice into 8 pieces and serve.

RASPBERRY MUFFINS

MAKES **6–8** MUFFINS

These light, fluffy muffins are a big hit for vegans and non-vegans alike.

DRY

1 cup whole wheat pastry flour

1 cup unbleached all-purpose flour

2 teaspoons baking powder

⅛ teaspoon sea salt

WET

⅓ cup safflower oil

½ cup maple syrup, or rice syrup and maple syrup combined

⅔ cup almond milk or soy milk

¼ cup apple juice

1 tablespoon orange zest

1 teaspoon vanilla extract

1 cup fresh or frozen raspberries, plus more for topping

1. Preheat oven to 350°F.
2. Sift both flours. Mix all dry ingredients in a large mixing bowl.
3. In a separate mixing bowl, mix all wet ingredients.
4. Add wet mixture to the dry mixture and mix with a spatula.
5. Add raspberries and mix gently.
6. Using an ice cream scoop, place the mixture in muffin molds. Add 1–2 raspberries on top of each muffin.
7. Bake for about 20–25 minutes until the surface turns light brown.
8. Check with a toothpick or bamboo stick. If it comes out clean, the muffins are done.
9. Let muffins cool on a cooling rack before serving.

VARIATIONS | You may also substitute orange juice for apple juice and blueberries for raspberries.

PECAN GLUTEN-FREE JAM THUMBPRINT COOKIES

MAKES 35–40 COOKIES

These moist, crunchy jam thumbprint cookies make gluten-free gems that everybody will love.

DRY

2½ cups pecans

1½ cups rolled oats

1 cup brown rice flour

1 teaspoon baking powder

WET

¾ cup maple syrup or rice syrup

¼ cup apple juice

¼ cup safflower oil

1 teaspoon vanilla extract

½ teaspoon sea salt

no-added-sugar, fruit-sweetened jam (strawberry, apricot, or blueberry)

1. Preheat oven to 300°F and place parchment paper on top of 2 large baking sheets.
2. Place pecans in a food processor and process until their texture is smooth and fine, with little nut grains remaining. Remove ground pecans and set aside.
3. Place rolled oats in the food processor and process until fine.
4. Combine ground rolled oats with ground pecans. Add flour and baking powder and mix well with a spatula.
5. In a separate mixing bowl, whisk together the wet ingredients until liquids emulsify.
6. Add wet mixture to the dry mixture. Using a spatula, mix until the dough texture becomes even.
7. With a small ice cream scoop, scoop about 1 tablespoon of dough onto prepared baking sheet.
8. Repeat step 7 with the rest of the dough. Make sure to leave a 1-inch space between cookies.
9. With your finger, make a small indentation in the middle of each piece of dough.
10. With a small spoon, ladle fruit jam into each indentation.
11. Bake in the oven for 15–20 minutes until they turn light brown on both top and bottom. Cookies burn easily, so check often after 10 minutes of baking.
12. Set aside to cool at room temperature before serving.

APPLE-BLUEBERRY CRISP

SERVES **6–8**

This warming baked dessert is simply prepared in a casserole dish—a perfect treat for a large group. Serve with AMAZAKE CREAM (page 269) if desired.

CRISP CRUMBLE

½ cup rolled oats

½ cup whole wheat pastry flour

½ cup brown rice flour

½ cup coarsely chopped walnuts

⅛ teaspoon sea salt

5 tablespoons safflower oil

3–4 tablespoons maple syrup

FRUIT FILLING

¾ cup apple juice

1 tablespoon kuzu

pinch of sea salt

1 teaspoon vanilla extract

2 apples (Gala, Honeycrisp, Pink Lady, or other sweet, firm type), cored and cut into very thin slices (2½ cups)

1 cup fresh or frozen blueberries

1. Preheat oven to 350°F.

2. In a large mixing bowl, combine rolled oats, flours, walnuts, and sea salt. Add safflower oil and mix using a fork. Add maple syrup. Using your hands, continue mixing to form crumbles.

3. In a separate mixing bowl, combine apple juice, kuzu, a pinch of sea salt, and vanilla extract. Completely dissolve kuzu in the liquid.

4. Place apple slices in an oven pan such as a casserole dish. Layer blueberries on top of the apple slices and pour the apple juice mixture over the fruit.

5. Place crumble mixture on top of the fruit filling and distribute evenly. Cover with casserole top or aluminum foil and bake in the oven for 30–40 minutes until it bubbles.

6. Remove cover and bake for about 10 more minutes until surface becomes golden.

7. Let sit for 15 minutes before serving. Serve while still warm or at room temperature.

VARIATIONS | The filling can be varied with different seasonal fruits, such as peaches, pears, and other kinds of berries. Substitute brown rice flour for whole wheat flour for a gluten-free crisp.

PECAN-CRANBERRY SCONES

MAKES 4–6 SCONES

These are hearty and satisfying vegan scones for everybody.

DRY

½ cup whole wheat pastry flour

½ cup unbleached white pastry flour

1 teaspoon baking powder

2 pinches of sea salt

WET

3 tablespoons safflower oil

1 tablespoon soy milk or other nondairy milk

2 tablespoons maple syrup

1 tablespoon orange juice

1 teaspoon orange zest

¼ cup coarsely chopped pecans

3 tablespoons coarsely chopped cranberries

nondairy milk, for coating

maple syrup, for coating

1. Preheat oven to 350°F. Prepare a baking sheet by lining with parchment paper.
2. Sift both flours into a medium mixing bowl. Add baking powder and sea salt.
3. In a separate mixing bowl, whisk together the wet ingredients until liquids emulsify.
4. Add wet mixture to the dry mixture. Using a spatula, mix until everything harmonizes together.
5. Add pecans and cranberries. Mix gently, folding evenly into the dough.
6. Use your hands to press the dough against the bowl and shape into a ball.
7. Place dough on a lightly floured cutting board and pat into a round shape 1 inch thick.
8. Using a sharp knife, cut dough into 4–6 triangles depending on your scone size preference.
9. Place each slice of dough on the prepared baking sheet. Coat the surface of each scone with milk using a pastry brush.
10. Bake for about 20 minutes until light brown.
11. Take out of the oven and coat the surface of each scone with maple syrup using a pastry brush.
12. Place back in the oven and bake for 5 minutes.
13. Take out of the oven. Let cool for 5 minutes and serve warm or at room temperature.

VARIATION | Vary the ingredients using raisins, blueberries, cherries, or almonds. For lighter, fluffier scones, use unbleached white pastry flour for all of the flour called for in the recipe.

CHERRY-AMAZAKE TART

SERVES 8 (MAKES A 9½-INCH TART)

The sweet, tangy flavor, the creamy texture of the filling, and the crunchy crust give this tart perfect harmony and a whiff of healthy decadence.

CRUST	AMAZAKE MIXTURE	CHERRY MIXTURE
½ cup rolled oats	¼ cup apple juice	10 ounces fresh or frozen cherries
1 cup pastry flour	2 tablespoons agar-agar flakes	¼ cup apple juice
½ cup brown rice flour	pinch of sea salt	1 tablespoon agar-agar flakes
¼ teaspoon sea salt	2 cups blended amazake	pinch of sea salt
¼ cup safflower oil		
2 tablespoons maple syrup		
2 tablespoons rice syrup		
¼ cup apple juice		

TO MAKE THE CRUST:

1. Preheat oven to 350°F.
2. In a large mixing bowl, combine rolled oats, flours, and sea salt. Mix well with a whisk.
3. In a separate mixing bowl, whisk together safflower oil, syrups, and apple juice until liquids emulsify.
4. Add wet mixture to the dry mixture. Using a spatula, mix until the texture of the dough becomes even.
5. Using your hands, place dough into a tart mold.
6. Bake in the oven for 15–20 minutes until the crust becomes a golden color.
7. Set aside to cool to room temperature.

TO MAKE THE AMAZAKE MIXTURE:

1. Place apple juice, agar-agar flakes, and sea salt in a saucepan.
2. Over a medium flame, bring to a boil, reduce flame to medium-low, and simmer for 4–5 minutes until agar-agar flakes are dissolved, stirring constantly.
3. Add amazake and stir until everything blends well.

TO MAKE THE CHERRY MIXTURE:

1. Blend cherries in a blender until smooth, making 1 cup. Set aside.
2. Place apple juice, agar-agar flakes, and sea salt in a saucepan.
3. Over a medium flame, bring to a boil, reduce flame to medium-low, and simmer for 4–5 minutes until agar-agar flakes are dissolved, stirring constantly.

4. Reduce flame to low. Add blended cherries and stir until everything blends well.

TO ASSEMBLE THE TART:

1. Alternate placing scoops of the amazake mixture and the cherry mixture on top of the crust, one scoop at a time, until the tart mold is filled to the top.
2. If you like, make swirl patterns or mandala art on top using a chopstick.
3. Let cool until the tart is set. Serve at room temperature or chilled.

CHEF'S TIP: *If using homemade amazake, see chef's tip in the recipe for* RASPBERRY-AMAZAKE MOUSSE *(page 243).*

APPLE PIE

Apple pie is an American classic. We enjoy this delicious, naturally sweetened dessert on Thanksgiving, during the winter holidays, and for birthdays and other special occasions.

APPLE FILLING

- 5–7 apples, cored and sliced into wedges (4–5 cups)
- ¼ cup apple juice
- 1 tablespoon maple syrup
- ¼ teaspoon sea salt
- ½ teaspoon cinnamon powder
- 1 tablespoon kuzu, dissolved in 2 tablespoons apple juice

DOUBLE CRUST

- 1¼ cups all-purpose flour
- 1¼ cups pastry flour
- ¼ teaspoon sea salt
- ½ cup safflower oil
- 2 tablespoons apple juice
- ¼ cup maple syrup, plus 2 tablespoons for glazing

TO MAKE THE APPLE FILLING:

1. Place apple slices, apple juice, maple syrup, and sea salt in a saucepan. Bring to a boil, reduce flame to low, and simmer for 5 minutes. Make sure the apple slices are slightly cooked but not mushy.
2. Add cinnamon and dissolved kuzu and simmer for a few minutes until the mixture thickens, stirring constantly.

TO MAKE THE DOUBLE CRUST:

1. Preheat oven to 350°F.
2. Place flours and sea salt in a large mixing bowl. Mix well with a whisk.
3. In a separate mixing bowl, whisk together safflower oil, apple juice, and ¼ cup of maple syrup until liquids emulsify.
4. Add wet mixture to the dry mixture. Using a spatula, mix until the dough texture becomes even. Cover the dough with plastic wrap and let stand for 15 minutes.
5. Divide the dough into two pieces. On lightly floured parchment paper, roll out the first half of the dough and form it into a disk that is slightly larger in diameter than the pie plate. Transfer the dough by lifting the parchment paper. Flip the parchment paper upside down so that the dough evenly fits into the pie plate, using it as the bottom-layer crust.
6. To make the top layer of the crust, roll out the second half of the dough the same way as the first half, this time forming a crust slightly smaller in diameter. Set aside.

1. Place apple filling on the bottom crust.
2. Lift the parchment paper with the top-layer crust. Flip the parchment paper upside down so that the dough evenly covers the apple filling.
3. Cut off any extra dough that hangs over the edges of the bottom crust.
4. Make an X-shaped incision about 2 inches wide in the top layer of the dough, with the center of the X in the center of the top layer. This allows the pie to breathe while it is baking.
5. Using your thumb and index finger, gently pinch the top layer of the dough around the edge of the crust, firmly sealing to create a well-shaped ridge.
6. Using the middle rack of the oven, bake for about 25 minutes until pie is slightly browned.
7. Meanwhile, combine remaining 2 tablespoons of maple syrup with 1 tablespoon of water to make a glaze.
8. Remove pie from oven and add glaze on top using a pastry brush.
9. Place pie back in the oven and bake for 15–20 more minutes. Apply the glaze once more toward the end of the cooking time. When golden brown, remove from oven.
10. Let cool completely on a cooling rack. Slice and serve.

AZUKI CHOCOLATE CAKE

MAKES A 7-INCH SQUARE CAKE

Inspired by Mitsuko Mikami's recipe, this is a great dessert to make when you have leftover azuki beans. The texture of azuki is similar to chocolate chips, making for a decadent dessert with a healthy touch.

DRY

2 cups all-purpose flour

⅓ cup cocoa powder

2 teaspoons baking powder

2 teaspoons grain coffee powder (optional)

WET

⅓ cup safflower oil

½ cup maple syrup

½ cup soy milk or other nondairy milk

¼ teaspoon sea salt

1 teaspoon vanilla extract

1 cup cooked azuki beans

coconut flakes, for topping

1. Preheat oven to 300°F. Line a 7-inch square baking pan with parchment paper.
2. Place dry ingredients in a large mixing bowl.
3. In a separate mixing bowl, whisk together wet ingredients until liquids emulsify.
4. Add azuki beans to the wet mixture.
5. Pour wet mixture into the dry mixture. Don't take too long during the mixing process, because the baking powder will lose its ability to rise.
6. Pour the batter into the baking pan. Sprinkle coconut flakes on top.
7. Bake for 25–35 minutes until the dough is baked all the way through and a toothpick inserted comes out clean.
8. Let cool for 30 minutes before serving.

TIRAMISU WITH CASHEW-AMAZAKE CREAM

SERVES **6–8** *(see photo on page 232)*

This luscious tiramisu has a smooth texture and a ricÚess from the cream and grain coffee syrup. Each bite melts in your mouth with joy.

SPONGE CAKE

1 cup unbleached pastry flour

1 cup all-purpose flour

1½ teaspoons baking powder

⅛ teaspoon sea salt

⅓ cup safflower oil

½ cup maple syrup

¾ cup apple juice

1 teaspoon vanilla extract

GRAIN COFFEE SYRUP

3 tablespoons grain coffee powder

1 tablespoon rice syrup

3 cups CASHEW-AMAZAKE CREAM (recipe follows), divided

cocoa powder, for topping

TO MAKE THE SPONGE CAKE:

1. Preheat oven to 350°F. Line a baking sheet (about 9 × 14) with parchment paper.
2. Sift flours, baking powder, and sea salt into a large mixing bowl and mix with a whisk.
3. In a separate mixing bowl, whisk together the safflower oil, maple syrup, apple juice, and vanilla extract until liquids emulsify.
4. Pour wet mixture into the dry mixture and mix well with a spatula.
5. Pour the batter onto the baking sheet. Using a spatula, spread batter about ⅓ inch in thickness on the baking sheet.
6. Bake for about 10–15 minutes until the color becomes golden and a toothpick inserted comes out clean.
7. Let cool completely to room temperature.

TO MAKE THE GRAIN COFFEE SYRUP:

1. Bring ⅔ cup of water to a boil. Add grain coffee powder and maple syrup and stir to dissolve.
2. Let cool to room temperature.

TO ASSEMBLE THE TIRAMISU:

1. Cut the crusty edges off the cake and slice the cake in half horizontally.
2. Place one of the sponge cake halves in a container (about 8 × 6 × 2), top side down. You may cut the cake into smaller squares to fit the entire surface of the container.

3. With a pastry brush, apply about half of the coffee syrup to the entire surface of the cake.
4. Spread 1½ cups of the cashew-amazake cream evenly on top, about ½-inch thick.
5. Place the second sponge cake half on top, top side down.
6. Repeat steps 3 and 4, ending with a cream layer.
7. Cover and let tiramisu sit in the refrigerator for at least 4 hours, preferably overnight.
8. Just before serving the tiramisu, sprinkle cocoa powder on top using a tea strainer. Cut into nice square pieces and serve.

CASHEW-AMAZAKE CREAM

MAKES 4 CUPS

This sweet and rich spread can be used as cake frosting or as a dessert topping.

2 cups raw cashews, soaked with 2 cups water overnight, drained and rinsed

2 tablespoons lemon juice, plus 1 teaspoon for blending

3 tablespoons maple syrup

1 teaspoon umeboshi vinegar

5 tablespoons agar-agar flakes

pinch of sea salt

2 cups blended amazake

1½ teaspoons vanilla extract

1 tablespoon lemon zest

1. In food processor, place cashews, ⅓ cup of water, 2 tablespoons of lemon juice, maple syrup, and umeboshi vinegar and blend until smooth.
2. In a saucepan, place ½ cup of water, agar-agar flakes, and sea salt. Bring to a boil over a medium-low flame, reduce flame to low, and simmer for 4–5 minutes until agar-agar flakes are completely dissolved, stirring constantly.
3. Slowly add amazake to the saucepan while stirring well.
4. Slowly bring back to a boil and add the cashew mixture and vanilla extract. Mix well with a whisk. Transfer the mixture to a heat-safe glass container and let cool to room temperature. Chill in refrigerator for 1–2 hours or until it sets.
5. Remove from refrigerator and blend mixture with remaining 1 teaspoon of lemon juice and lemon zest in a food processor until the texture is smooth and creamy.
6. Store leftover cream in a glass jar and keep in the refrigerator for 3–4 days.

ALMOND CREAM

MAKES 2 CUPS

Almond cream is rich and delicious, a perfect topping, spread, or filling for snacks and desserts.

1 cup raw almonds, soaked with 2 cups water overnight

3 tablespoons maple syrup

pinch of sea salt

1 teaspoon vanilla extract

1. Drain the almonds and peel skin.
2. Blend peeled almonds and 1 cup of water in a food processor for 3–4 minutes until smooth (if using high-speed blender, blend for 2 minutes).
3. Place the almond mixture, maple syrup, and sea salt in a saucepan and slowly bring to a boil over low flame, stirring gently.
4. Add vanilla extract and stir to mix. Let cool to room temperature and chill in the refrigerator.
5. Store leftover cream in a glass jar and keep in the refrigerator for 3–4 days.

CASHEW CREAM

MAKES 2 CUPS

Cashew cream makes a delicious topping, spread, or frosting for desserts and snacks. It is easy to make and gives a rich, satisfying taste.

1 cup cashews, soaked with 1 cup water overnight and drained

⅓ cup apple juice

2 tablespoons lemon juice

⅓ cup maple syrup

¼ teaspoon umeboshi vinegar

1 teaspoon vanilla extract

1. In a blender or food processor, place soaked cashews, apple juice, lemon juice, maple syrup, umeboshi vinegar, and vanilla extract.
2. Blend well until smooth.
3. Store leftover cream in a glass jar and keep in the refrigerator for 3–4 days.

AMAZAKE CREAM

MAKES 2½ CUPS

This is a simple version of a white cream that makes a sweet, smooth topping for cakes and mousses.

4 tablespoons agar-agar flakes

3 tablespoons brown rice syrup

few pinches of sea salt

2 cups blended amazake

1 tablespoon kuzu, dissolved in 2 tablespoons cold water

1 teaspoon vanilla extract

1 tablespoon lemon zest

1. Combine 1 cup of water and agar-agar flakes in a saucepan. Bring to a boil over a medium flame, reduce flame to low, and simmer for 4–5 minutes until agar-agar flakes are completely dissolved, stirring constantly.

2. Add brown rice syrup and sea salt and let the syrup completely melt.

3. Slowly add amazake and continue to stir for a few minutes.

4. Add dissolved kuzu and vanilla extract and stir while simmering for a few more minutes.

5. Transfer into a heat-safe glass container and let cool to room temperature. Then refrigerate for 1–2 hours until it sets.

6. Blend the mixture in a food processor until smooth.

7. Add lemon zest. Taste, adjusting flavor if necessary.

8. Store leftover cream in a glass jar and keep in the refrigerator for 3–4 days.

Bancha Twig Tea
(see recipe on page 273)

REFRESHING
BEVERAGES AND
NATURAL REMEDIES

"We sent down water from heaven as a blessing and caused thereby gardens and harvest grain to grow, and tall palm trees with spathes heaped up, a provision for our servants; and revived thereby a barren land. Like that shall the resurrection be."
—THE QUR'AN

PREFERRED FOR ITS LIGHT, UPWARD ENERGY, CLEAR, FRESH, NATURAL SPRING WATER is enjoyed by people around the world as their main daily source of drinking and cooking water. In modern urban areas, bottled spring water is a thriving industry as people turn away from chemicalized municipal tap water toward healthier foods and beverages.

Natural spring water that is alive and moving carries strong ki, or natural electromagnetic energy. Water facilitates digestion and absorption, balances salt and other minerals in the body, and contributes to the proper functioning of the kidneys, bladder, blood, lymph, and all other bodily systems and functions. Human beings consist of about 70 percent water, and obtaining the highest-quality water for drinking and cooking is a top priority.

The quality of spring water differs widely, and there are generally no governmental standards. Some spring water is too high in minerals and trace elements, others too low. Some is clear, others cloudy or ruddy. Spring water is ideally stored in glass bottles, though plastic is acceptable if not left unused indefinitely, which allows chemicals to seep into the container. Municipal tap water usually contains chlorine, fluoride, and other potentially hazardous chemicals, as well as pesticide residues, detergents, nitrates, and heavy metals. Distilled water lacks nutrients, is low in vitality, and gives low energy. Mineral, carbonate, or bubbling waters make a nice party drink on occasion but are not recommended for regular use. Well water is a good alternative to spring water but is often harder and heavier and contains more trace minerals because it comes from deeper underground. If spring or well water is not available or too costly, filtered tap water is usually the best alternative. There are a variety of water filters, with each having its pros and cons.

Besides water, there are several beverages commonly consumed in macrobiotic households. These include *bancha* twig tea, roasted barley tea, and others.

Vegetable and Fruit Juices

Juice and cider are tasty and relaxing, but, as a concentrated beverage, up to ten or more apples or other fruits may be used to make one serving. On a daily basis, this can take a toll on the kidneys and bladder, so juice is best consumed in moderation, only few times a week. Vegetable juice is less stressful than fruit juice, and temperate-climate produce is preferable to tropical in a four-season climate.

BANCHA TWIG TEA

MAKES **4** CUPS *(see photo on page 270)*

Calm, soothing, and nutrient rich, bancha twig tea (or *kukicha*, as it is also known) is one of the most healthful daily beverages on the planet. Harvested from the twigs of the tea bush, it is the main drink in many Asian, macrobiotic, and natural foods households.

Bancha twig tea has a mild, relaxing effect on digestion, blood quality, and the mind and emotions. It is safe for children and infants to drink. The twigs of the tea bush have virtually no caffeine or tannins (astringent compounds that give a dry and puckery feeling in the mouth).

1 tablespoon bancha twigs

1. In a large cooking pot, place bancha twigs and 1 quart of water and bring to a boil. Reduce flame to low and simmer for 4–5 minutes.
2. Pour tea into cups through a tea strainer and serve.

CHEF'S TIP: *Twigs in strainer may be returned to teapot and used several times, adding a few fresh twigs each time.*

ROASTED BARLEY TEA

MAKES **6** CUPS

Roasted barley tea helps melt away animal fat from the body and reduce fever. It is also very relaxing, especially in the spring or summer. This tea can also be purchased preroasted from select natural foods stores, Asian/Japanese stores, and online.

1 cup uncooked barley

1. Dry roast barley in a skillet over medium flame for 10 minutes until barley turns an even golden color. Stir and shake pan occasionally to prevent burning.
2. In a large cooking pot, bring 1 quart of water to a boil. Add roasted barley, reduce flame to low, and simmer for 15–20 minutes.
3. Pour tea into cups through a tea strainer and serve.

VARIATION | Millet and other whole grains may be used to make teas in this way.

CORN SILK TEA

MAKES 1 CUP

Corn silk tea is good for discharging fat and cholesterol and is effective as a natural diuretic. Be sure to purchase certified organic corn, since most corn is genetically engineered.

⅓ cup dried corn silk

1. In a medium cooking pot, bring 1 cup of water to a boil. Add corn silk, reduce flame to low, and simmer for 5 minutes.
2. Strain and drink hot.

CHEF'S TIP: *To dry corn silk, remove corn silk from corncobs. Lay out the corn silk on a tray kept in a cool, dry area until corn silk is completely dried. Corn silk tea may be prepared from teabags purchased in natural food stores.*

SWEET VEGETABLE DRINK

MAKES 4–6 CUPS

This naturally sweet drink is made from four sweet vegetables and is unseasoned. It helps satisfy the desire or craving for a sweet taste and for overall relaxation. We sometimes make this drink in the early afternoon for our students and clients, especially those who have hypoglycemia, or chronic low blood sugar, which dips at this time of day. Note: no salt or other seasoning is used in this drink.

¼ cup finely diced onion

¼ cup finely diced carrots

¼ cup finely diced cabbage

¼ cup finely diced winter squash

1. In a large pot, place vegetables and 4 cups of water. Bring to a boil over medium flame, cover, and reduce flame to low. Simmer for 20–30 minutes.
2. Strain the vegetables from the broth. Drink the broth hot or at room temperature.

VARIATION | For a sweeter drink, substitute corn, sweet potato, or yam for carrot.

CHEF'S TIP: *This sweet vegetable drink may be kept in the refrigerator for several days and heated before serving.*

"Let food be thy medicine and thy medicine be food."
—HIPPOCRATES

IN MACROBIOTIC HEALTH CARE, ORDINARY, EVERYDAY FOODS ARE USED TO BALANCE an overly yin or yang condition or for first aid. The following remedies are safe, simple, inexpensive, and effective. For further information, including hundreds of home remedies, please see *Macrobiotic Home Remedies* by Michio Kushi with Marc Van Cauwenberghe and Alex Jack.

KITCHEN FIRST AID FOR CUTS, BURNS, AND BRUISES

For simple nicks and cuts, such as those obtained while cutting vegetables, wash under running water or clean with salty water. Then take a small piece of nori seaweed and place it around the affected finger, applying pressure to staunch the bleeding.

Additionally, eating 1 teaspoon of *gomashio* will also help minimize external bleeding. Avoid taking fluids or applying anything cold on the affected area. For cuts requiring stitches, be sure to consult a physician or professional healthcare provider.

For minor burns or scalds, apply cold saltwater to the affected area, or cover with a linen or paper towel drenched with this water. Continue this treatment until the pain disappears. If cold saltwater is unavailable, cover with cool large green leaves (such as collard greens).

It is advisable to always keep nori, tofu, leafy greens, and daikon on hand for emergencies like these, as well as many other common household mishaps. For severe wounds or injuries, consult a physician.

CARROT-DAIKON DRINK

MAKES 2 CUPS

This drink helps to dissolve solidified fat deposits existing deep within the body. It is a major macrobiotic remedy to help prevent or relieve heart disease, many cancers, and other disorders caused by excessive saturated fat and oil in meat, poultry, and dairy products. The daikon melts the hardened accumulations from within and discharges it primarily through the urine. The carrots, shoyu, nori, and umeboshi (all more yang) help to balance the daikon (more yin).

⅓–½ cup finely grated carrots

½ cup finely grated daikon

⅓ sheet nori

¼–½ umeboshi plum, minced

several drops of shoyu

1. In a saucepan, place carrots and daikon. Add nori and umeboshi plum.
2. Add 1 cup of water and bring to a gentle boil.
3. Simmer for about 3 minutes and add a few drops of shoyu toward the end.
4. Serve the hot broth with vegetables. Leftover drink can be kept in the refrigerator and served warm the next day.

LEAFY GREENS JUICE

MAKES 2 CUPS

Leafy greens juice can be used to dissolve heavy, stagnated protein and animal fat.

1 cup leafy greens (such as ½ cup finely chopped kale and ½ cup finely chopped collard greens)

pinch of sea salt or a few drops of shoyu

1. In a large pot, place vegetables and 2 cups of water.
2. Bring to a gentle boil and simmer for 3–5 minutes.
3. Add a pinch of sea salt or a few drops of shoyu toward the end of simmering and stir.
4. Strain out vegetables. Drink hot or at room temperature. Consume within one day.

CHEF'S TIP: *The leafy green vegetables may be reused in cooking or composted.*

SHIITAKE MUSHROOM TEA

MAKES 1 CUP

Shiitake mushrooms are very relaxing. This tea is traditionally used to reduce fever, dissolve animal-based fat, and help relax a contracted or tense condition.

1 dried shiitake mushroom

pinch of sea salt or several drops of shoyu

1. Soak mushroom in 1 cup of water for 20 minutes.
2. When mushroom is soft, chop finely.
3. Place mushroom and soaking water into a saucepan, bring to a boil, reduce flame to medium-low, and simmer gently for 10–15 minutes.
4. Add a pinch of sea salt or a few drops of shoyu toward the end. Drink hot.

SHOYU-BANCHA TEA

MAKES 1 CUP

This tea (also known as *sho-ban*) is used to strengthen the blood and neutralize an overly acidic condition, relieve fatigue, ease headaches due to the overconsumption of simple sugars and/or fruit juice, and stimulate circulation. This tea and UME-SHO BANCHA (below) also help prevent infections.

1 teaspoon shoyu

1 cup hot BANCHA TWIG TEA (page 273)

1. Place shoyu in a cup and pour hot bancha twig tea over it.
2. Stir and drink hot.

UME-SHO BANCHA

MAKES 1 CUP

This gently alkalizing tea is used to strengthen the blood; regulate digestion and circulation; relieve fatigue and weakness; and to obtain relief from the overconsumption of simple sugars, fruit, fruit juices, or other acid-forming foods or beverages.

¼–½ umeboshi plum, minced

few drops of shoyu

1 cup hot BANCHA TWIG TEA (page 273)

1. Place umeboshi plum in a cup with the shoyu.
2. Pour hot bancha twig tea into the cup and stir well. Drink hot.

UME-SHO KUZU

MAKES 1 CUP

Ume-sho kuzu is a standard macrobiotic drink used to strengthen digestion, restore energy, reduce inflammation, and help the body discharge acidity. It is slightly stronger and more soothing than *ume-sho bancha*.

1 heaping teaspoon kuzu, dissolved in 1 tablespoon cold water

¼–½ umeboshi plum, minced

several drops of shoyu

1. In a saucepan, place the dissolved kuzu and 1 cup of water.
2. Bring to a boil over a medium flame, stirring constantly to avoid lumping, until the liquid becomes translucent. Reduce flame to low.
3. Add the umeboshi plum and several drops of shoyu (up to 1 teaspoon) and stir gently. Simmer for 2–3 minutes. Drink hot.

VARIATION | Adding a little grated ginger to *ume-sho kuzu* is even more effective in activating digestion and warming the body.

AME KUZU

MAKES 1 CUP

Brown rice syrup, or *ame*, added to kuzu tea produces a sweet, relaxing beverage that helps relieve tension and reduce the craving for sweets, simple sugars, and alcohol. Taken before bed, it helps promote deep, relaxing sleep.

1 heaping teaspoon kuzu, dissolved in 1 tablespoon cold water

1 tablespoon brown rice syrup

1. In a saucepan, place 1 cup of water and add the dissolved kuzu, mixing thoroughly.
2. Place over a medium flame and bring to a boil. Reduce flame to medium-low and stir constantly with a wooden spoon to prevent clumping.
3. Add brown rice syrup to the hot liquid, and stir to dissolve.
4. When the kuzu becomes thick and clear, pour into a cup or bowl and drink hot.

VARIATION | You may substitute organic apple juice for water in the recipe and omit the rice syrup.

BLACK SOYBEAN TEA

MAKES 1–2 CUPS

Black soybean tea helps strengthen female reproductive health. It helps warm the body and create smooth and regular elimination. It also helps relieve coughing and mucus in the throat.

1 cup black soybeans

1. Place soybeans in a pot, add 4–6 cups of water, and bring to a boil.
2. Reduce flame to medium-low, cover, and simmer for 30–45 minutes.
3. Strain out the beans and drink 1–2 cups of the tea while hot.
4. Store leftover tea in a jar and keep in the refrigerator for 2 days. Heat before drinking.

VARIATIONS | You may continue cooking the beans with additional water until soft and edible. Try adding chopped carrots and sweet winter squash and shoyu as a seasoning to make as a side dish.

LOTUS ROOT TEA

Lotus root tea helps eliminate mucus in the respiratory system and ease coughing.

3-inch long section of fresh lotus root (2-inch diameter)

pinch of sea salt or few drops of shoyu

1. Wash the root and grate into fine pulp. Place pulp in a piece of cheesecloth and squeeze juice into a bowl. You may also place the gratings in your palm and squeeze the juice with your fingers, making ½ cup of lotus root juice total.

2. Place lotus juice in a saucepan with ½ cup of water. Add a pinch of sea salt or a few drops of shoyu.

3. Bring to a boil and reduce flame to low. Let simmer gently on a low flame for 2–3 minutes.

4. Drink hot. The tea should be thick and creamy.

VARIATION | You may also add a few drops of grated ginger juice toward the end if your condition permits, to warm the body and loosen stagnation. This tea is most effective when prepared from fresh lotus root, but if fresh lotus is not available, you may use dried lotus root or lotus root powder, available at select natural food stores.

LEAFY GREEN COMPRESS

The leaves of large leafy green vegetables (such as collards) are very helpful to cool down fevers, neutralize inflammation, and relieve burns and bruises. Often just putting big leaves on the head, chest, or arms will provide immediate relief. This compress is used to cool down quickly, and the leaves can be dipped in cold water and reused.

several collard, kale, or napa cabbage leaves

1. Carefully remove several whole leaves from a bunch of collards, kale, or napa cabbage.

2. Flatten slightly by scoring the spine horizontally with a vegetable knife.

3. Apply leaves two layers thick on the affected area. They may be held on for 10–15 minutes or longer (up to 1–2 hours in some cases) by wrapping with a piece of cheesecloth. As the leaves become heated, they may be cooled in cold water and reused or replaced with fresh leaves.

DAIKON POULTICE

For a tooth problem caused by minor inflammation, a daikon poultice may be helpful. This application is effective for hot, inflammatory conditions. For other teeth problems, a hot compress may be more effective. For further information, please see *Macrobiotic Home Remedies* by Michio Kushi with Marc Van Cauwenberghe and Alex Jack.

1 ounce fresh daikon, grated

1. Place daikon in a 6-inch square piece of cheesecloth and tie with a string to make a small poultice.
2. Place poultice over the cheek, the area above or below the lip, or other affected areas.
3. Hold for 5–10 minutes and often the pain will go away or lessen. Repeat several times during the day.

Neutralizing Extremes

Offsetting the harmful effects of extreme foods is an important part of the macrobiotic way of eating. The following suggestions may be helpful:

- **Too much sugar or chocolate, commonly leading to a frontal headache:** Take one or two servings of miso soup, *ume-sho bancha*, or a small handful of *gomashio*. Craving sugar and sweets is commonly the result of hypoglycemia, or chronic low blood sugar. The underlying cause is consuming too many heavy animal foods or baked foods that tighten the pancreas. To relax this organ and raise blood sugar levels, decrease these items and use grain-based sweeteners, such as brown rice syrup and barley malt, which are more stabilizing than sugar and other simple sweets that cause precipitous swings in mood.
- **Too much oil and fat, commonly leading to a headache on the sides of the head:** Take a small volume of raw or heated grated daikon with a few drops of shoyu.
- **Too much salt, salty foods, or animal foods, commonly leading to a headache in the back of the head:** Take one small cup of shiitake tea or warm apple juice.
- **Too much alcohol:** Take half to one umeboshi plum dissolved in one cup of *bancha* twig tea.
- **Insomnia:** If you wake in the night after about 2 a.m. and can't go back to sleep, your condition is generally too yang. Take one small cup of warm apple juice or ginger tea (squeezing the oil from one teaspoon of grated fresh ginger into a cup of hot water). If you can't fall asleep from about 10 p.m. to 2 a.m., your condition is probably too yin. Take one cup of *bancha* twig tea with a few drops of shoyu, chew a few mouthfuls of brown rice, or take a spoonful of *gomashio*.

RESOURCES

EDUCATION

Classes in macrobiotics are offered by the following educational centers, including programs for future teachers and chefs with training in cooking, healthcare, and other subjects; summer conferences; and weekend seminars for the general public:

Planetary Health, Inc. Sponsor of Amberwaves, a grassroots network to protect rice, wheat, and other grains from genetic engineering and climate change and keep America and the planet beautiful. Offers programs and seminars by Alex Jack, Sachi Kato, and other macrobiotic teachers and chefs and sponsors of the Macrobiotic Summer Conference, Macrobiotic Wellness Retreat, and Planetary Health Institute.

Box 487, Becket, MA 01223 | Tel: 413-623-0012
Websites: www.macrobioticwellnessretreat.com | www.macrobioticsummerconference.com
www.makropedia.com | Email: shenwa26@yahoo.com

Kushi Institute of Europe. Cofounded and directed by Wieke Nelissen.

Weteringschans 65, 1017RX Amsterdam, The Netherlands | Tel: 011 31 20 625 7513
Website: www.macrobiotics.nl | Email: kushi@macrobiotics.nl

Kushi Macrobiotic School. An affiliated school in Tokyo led by Patricio Garcia de Parades.

3-14-16 Nishihara, Shibuya-ku, Tokyo 151-0066, Japan | Tel: +81-3-6326-6746
Website: www.kushischool.jp | Email: info@kushischool.jp

Nicola and David McCarthy. Offering Kushi Levels south of London.

Haywards Heath, West Sussex, RH16 4 LL, UK | Tel: 07710 805683
Website: www.kushischool.uk | Email: info@kushischool.uk

MACROBIOTIC COUNSELING

Please contact the authors regarding macrobiotic dietary and health consultations.

Sachi Kato gives private cooking classes and lectures, serves as a traveling macrobiotic chef, and gives consultations in person, by phone, or via Skype.

Contact: www.macrobiotic.sachikato.com | sachikato@gmail.com

Alex Jack lectures widely on diet, health, and the environment and gives personal macrobiotic dietary health and way of life consultations in person, by phone, or via Skype.

Contact: shenwa26@yahoo.com

MACROBIOTIC FOOD AND MAIL-ORDER COMPANIES

Eden Food Company is the leading macrobiotic food manufacturer and distributor in the United States. Many of its products are available through mail order.

Website: edenfoods.com

Gold Mine Natural Foods, a macrobiotic distributor in San Diego, CA, specializes in heirloom grains, beans, and seeds.

Website: goldminenaturalfoods.com

Natural Import Company, a macrobiotic distributor in Asheville, NC.

Website: naturalimport.com

Rhapsody is a macrobiotic food company in Vermont that makes organic tempeh, miso, amazake, *natto*, rice milk, vegan egg rolls, and other products.

Website: rhapsodynaturalfoods.com

Maine Coast Sea Vegetable is a macrobiotic food company in Maine that harvests alaria (wakame), laver (nori), kelp, and other sea vegetables from the Atlantic Ocean.

Website: www.seaveg.com

Maine Seaweed is a macrobiotic-oriented sea vegetable company run by Larch Hanson.

Website: theseaweedman.com

Si Sea Salt is harvested from Pacific Ocean waters off the coast of Baja's Southern California.

Website: www.sisalt.com

South River Miso, a macrobiotic company in western Massachusetts, makes a variety of misos, including barley, brown rice, dandelion and leek, azuki bean, chickpea, and millet.

Website: www.southrivermiso.com.

BIBLIOGRAPHY

Andrus, Christian Elwell, and Ben Rooney. *The Rice Revolution: Growing Organic Rice in New England*. Becket, MA: Amberwaves Press, 2017.

Kushi, Aveline, with Alex Jack. *Aveline Kushi's Complete Guide to Macrobiotic Cooking*. New York: Time-Warner, 1985.

Kushi, Michio with Alex Jack. *The Book of Macrobiotics: The Universal Way of Health and Happiness*. Garden City Park, NY: Square One Publishers, 2012.

_____. *The Cancer Prevention Diet*. New York: St. Martin's, 1983.

_____. *The Macrobiotic Path to Total Health*. New York: Ballantine, 2002.

_____. *One Peaceful World: Creating a Healthy Mind, Home, and World Community*. New York: Square One Publishers, 2017.

Kushi, Michio, with Marc Van Cauwenberge and Alex Jack. *Macrobiotic Home Remedies*. New York: Square One Publishers, 2013.

Periodicals

Amberwaves. Planetary Health. Becket, MA. A quarterly journal featuring articles by Alex Jack, Sachi Kato, and other macrobiotic teachers. www.amberwaves.com.

Macrobiotics Today. George Ohsawa Macrobiotic Foundation. Chico, CA. www.Ohsawamacrobiotics.com.

ACKNOWLEDGMENTS

We would like to express our heartfelt gratitude to:

Glenn Yeffeth of BenBella Books for presenting us with the opportunity to write a cookbook. The BenBella team of Leah, Laurel, Adrienne, Vy, Heather, Sarah, Alicia, and Jessika demonstrated incredible professionalism and steadfast guidance for the duration of the editing and publishing process.

Our literary agent, Jennifer Lyons. Her passion for promoting works that help people advance toward better health and greater happiness allowed this book to materialize.

From Alex Jack:

I would like to express my deepest gratitude to:

My parents, Homer and Esther, for instilling within me the ideals of peace and justice.

Michio and Aveline Kushi, my teachers, for their clarity, guidance, and encouragement.

My grandmother Cissy for bringing me up to honor natural foods.

My daughter Mariya, whom Michio endearingly nicknamed the Tartar Princess, for her love, kindness, and wonderful meals that sustained me through this project.

My sister Lucy, her companion Stan, and children, Michael and Molly, for their love and support.

My fellow teachers, counselors, and chefs, especially Edward Esko, Naomi Ichikawa Esko, and Bettina Zumdick, as well as students, clients, and friends, who have strengthened my understanding and practice.

And most of all, Sachi Kato, my student, teaching partner, and coauthor, my heartfelt appreciation for her bright spirit, peaceful mind, and light, creative touch.

From Sachi Kato:

I would like to express my deepest gratitude to:

My parents, Masakatsu and Emiko Kato, and my entire family in Japan for bringing me into this world, providing me with unconditional love, and always supporting me in my journey to achieve my dreams.

My husband, Travis, and my mother-in law, Carole, for their loyal support in its many shapes and forms.

My wonderful friends: Manuela, Kumi, Emi, Big Meg & Little Meg, Taeko, Susan, Claudia, Sommer, Naomi, and Kimiko, who inspire me to be who I am. Sharing lovely meals and cooking together with such amazing friends stirred my soul to author this cookbook.

Patricio Garcia de Paredes, Warren Kramer, Verne Varona, Edward Esko, Bettina Zumdick, Wieke and Adelbert Nelissen, Nadine Barner, Sanae Suzuki, and the many other macrobiotic chefs, teachers, and mentors who contributed their talents and their wisdom to my macrobiotic practice. They empowered me to reach out to others and share my knowledge through this cookbook.

My wonderful recipe testers, Yuri, Azusa, Donna, and my beloved friends and kitchen crew at Kushi Institute for expressing enthusiastic support and pure enjoyment of the food; it filled my heart with creative force.

Inaka Natural Foods Restaurant, whose delicious meals and wonderful community served as catalysts for my initial pursuit of studying macrobiotic cooking and philosophy.

Above all, Alex Jack, my honored mentor and coauthor of this cookbook, for his continuous encouragement and collaboration in making this book, and for his years of dedication to planetary health and world peace.

ABOUT THE AUTHORS

ALEX JACK is founder and president of Planetary Health, Inc.; sponsor of Amberwaves, a grassroots network devoted to promoting whole grains and other natural foods; and codirector of the Macrobiotic Summer Conference. He has helped introduce macrobiotics to China and Russia and has written many books with Michio and Aveline Kushi, including *The Cancer Prevention Diet*, *Diet for a Strong Heart*, *Aveline Kushi's Complete Guide to Macrobiotic Cooking*, *The Macrobiotic Path to Total Health*, and *The Book of Macrobiotics*. He also edited the Wheaten Garland editions of *Hamlet* and *As You Like It*.

Alex taught macrobiotic philosophy, healthcare, diagnosis, and cooking at Kushi Institute, where he served as executive director and chairman of the faculty. He has presented at the Cardiology Institute in St. Petersburg, the Zen Temple in Beijing, Shakespeare's New Globe Theatre in London, and the Rosas contemporary dance company in Brussels. He lives in the Berkshires.

Contact: shenwa26@yahoo.com

SACHI KATO grew up in a multigenerational household in Gifu, Japan, where she learned traditional methods of food harvesting and preparation from her family members.

Sachi trained and worked as a macrobiotic chef at Kushi Institutes in America, Japan, and Europe. She completed the comprehensive Macrobiotic Leadership Program, in which she studied cooking, healing, philosophy, and Oriental diagnosis. Sachi has since taught classes in these subjects at the Kushi Institute, as well as to the public in California, New York, and Japan.

While her dishes possess a Japanese sensibility and are rooted in macrobiotic practice, Sachi continually finds inspiration for her cooking from her international community and its many rich culinary traditions. As a result, she gratefully adopts cooking tecÚiques and ingredients from her planetary neighbors to innovate original recipes, as well as to create new versions of many well-known classics.

Employing her professional photography skills to capture the vibrant images of the dishes that appear in the pages of this cookbook, Sachi contributes her efforts as both a visual and culinary artist. She happily shares these gifts from nature which are steeped in the awareness that real nourishment and amazing health start with home cooking.

Sachi is currently based in the San Francisco Bay Area.

Contact: www.sachikato.com / sachikato@gmail.com

INDEX